D0790965

Uncle John's
BATHROOM PUZZLER.
HANGMAN-a-GRAMS

PORTABLE
PRESS

Bathroom Readers' Institute
Ashland, Oregon, and San Diego, California

UNCLE JOHN'S BATHROOM PUZZLER

HANGMAN-A-GRAMS

For information, write...
The Bathroom Readers' Institute
P.O. Box 1117, Ashland, OR 97520
www.bathroomreader.com
E-mail: mail@bathroomreader.com

Design by Lidija Tomas, Studio 4D
Cover by Rob Davis

ISBN-13: 978-1-60710-500-8

Printed in the United States of America
First printing: May 2012

1 2 3 4 5   16 15 14 13 12

THANK YOU!

The Bathroom Readers' Institute sincerely thanks the following people whose advice, assistance, and hard work made this book possible.

Gordon Javna

Stephanie Spadaccini

Jay Newman

Melinda Allman

Myles Callum

JoAnn Padgett

Brian Boone

Kim Griswell

Lidija Tomas

Rob Davis

Monica Maestas

Ginger Winters

Jennifer Frederick

Annie Lam

Trina Hedgpeth

Amy Miller

Lilian Nordland

William Dooling

Stan Sydley (It's an anagram.)

Uncle Henry and Aunt Em

Jules Herbert

Albert Einstein

Felix the Wonder Dog

Thomas Crapper

HANGMAN-A-GRAMS

Our version of Hangman is nearly the same as the game you've probably played before—only in this case, you can play alone. And everything you need is on these pages, except of course, for a pencil or pen.

THE SET-UP

Each left-hand page consists of a WORD LIST with blanks to be filled in (we've included all the vowels—A, E, I, O, U—and we've even thrown in Y to help you along). Below the list, you'll find all the letters you'll need to complete the words. But just in case you get stumped, we've provided a clue for each word in the CLUE SECTION, starting on page 202.

GET A CLUE!

We've set up the CLUE SECTION to make it easier for you to find the clue you're looking for—and to make it harder for you to accidentally see the other words in that particular word list. The clues are listed according to their number in the list: All the #1 words are in the same section and so on.

The clue might be anything: the first letter of the word, a definition of the word, an anagram of the word, another word that's contained in the word, or even a bit of trivia that might give you a hint.

Example: Let's say you're working on WORD LIST 17 and you've figured out a couple of the words, but get stumped on word #4. Just go to the page listed to the right of word #4 and scan down the page for WORD LIST 17 and/or the title of the list. There's your clue!

THE HANGMAN

And that's where the Hangman comes in. Each word list is accompanied by a diagram of a typical HANGMAN game. Every time you use a clue, you have to "pay" for it by filling in one piece of the little guy's body. The most common method is in this order—head, torso, arm, arm, leg, leg—but feel free to in the lines in any order you like.

TO SCORE OR NOT TO SCORE

Optional: This is for those of you who like even *more* of a challenge. Notice the SCORE box in the lower right corner of each Hangman page.

- If you complete a list without using any clues, write a zero in the SCORE box.
- If you had to use any clues, write in the number of clues you used in the box (1–6) Yes, there are eight words in each list—but you're allowed only a maximum of six clues if you're going to keep score.
- When you've completed all 100 word lists to the best of your ability, add all the numbers up: 0 being the best score you can get, 600 being the worst. Then compare yourself with our rating system.

0–100: The only thing you're guilty of is being a genius!

101–200: You have a way with words. We find you not guilty.

201–300: Pretty smart, but in need of a retrial.

301–400: Guilty. But you can always appeal to Judge Uncle John.

401–500: The governor called with a last-minute reprieve.

501–600: We're throwing a lynching party, and you're the guest of honor.

So have fun, and best of luck to you and the little guys inside!

—Uncle John and the BRI staff

1

THE PLANETS

1. M A R S   *clue on page 202*

2. E A _ _ _   *clue on page 210*

3. _ E _ U _   *clue on page 219*

4. _ A _ U _ _   *clue on page 227*

5. U _ A _ U _   *clue on page 236*

6. _ U _ I _ E _   *clue on page 244*

7. _ E _ _ U _ Y   *clue on page 253*

8. _ E _ _ U _ E   *clue on page 261*

```
C H J M N P R S T V
    M N P R S T
        N   R S T
        N   R S T
        N   R
            R
            R
```

The Mt. Palomar telescope can see objects 7,038,835,200,000,000,000,000 miles away.

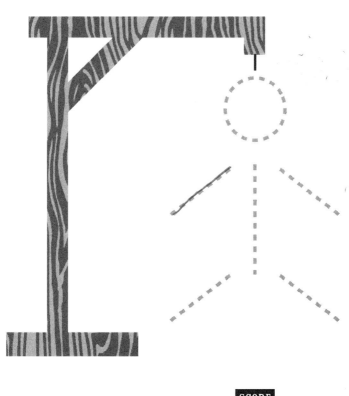

Answers on page 270

SCORE

The impact of the 1969 moon landing caused the moon's surface to vibrate for 55 minutes.

WORDS THAT START WITH G

1 _ U _ U

clue on page 202

2 _ A U _ E

clue on page 210

3 _ O A _ E E

clue on page 219

4 _ O A _ I E

clue on page 227

5 _ Y _ _ U _

clue on page 236

6 _ I _ A _ _ E

clue on page 244

7 _ E _ _ _ O _ E

clue on page 253

8 _ Y _ _ A _ I U _

clue on page 261

```
F G L M N P R S T Z
F G   M N   R S T
  G   M       S
  G   M
  G
  G
  G
  G
```

What do you call a person who will believe anything? A *gobemouche*.

Answers on page 270

SCORE

They may sound Japanese, but Ginsu knives were actually invented in Ohio.

WAYS TO SAY HI AND BYE

1. _ I A O   *clue on page 202*

2. A _ I O _   *clue on page 210*

3. A _ O _ A   *clue on page 219*

4. _ Y E - _ Y E   *clue on page 227*

5. _ O O _ _ E _   *clue on page 236*

6. _ O _ _ _ E E _   *clue on page 244*

7. _ A Y O _ A _ A   *clue on page 253*

8. _ _ E E _ I   *clue on page 261*

```
B C D G H L N P R S T
B   D G   L N   R S T
    D G         S
    D           S
                S
```

Worldwide, the most common form of greeting is a kiss.

Answers on page 270

Myron Lowery, the mayor of Memphis, TN, "fist-bumped" the visiting Dalai Lama.

WORDS THAT START WITH T

1   _ O _ U   *clue on page 202*

2   _ I A _ A   *clue on page 210*

3   _ A _ _ U _   *clue on page 219*

4   _ U _ E _ O   *clue on page 227*

5   _ A _ I O _ A   *clue on page 236*

6   _ E _ I O U _   *clue on page 244*

7   _ E _ _ U _ A   *clue on page 253*

8   _ A _ I _ E _ _ Y   *clue on page 261*

```
C D F L M P R S T X
C D     M P R   T X
  D     M   R   T
                T
                T
                T
                T
                T
```

Toblerone is a portmanteau of the creator's name, Theodor Tobler, and...

Answers on page 270

...torrone, an Italian word for a type of nougat.

STAR SIGNS

1. __ E O   *clue on page 202*

2. A __ I E __   *clue on page 210*

3. __ I __ __ O   *clue on page 219*

4. __ I __ __ E __   *clue on page 227*

5. __ A U __ U __   *clue on page 236*

6. A __ U A __ I U __   *clue on page 244*

7. __ A __ __ I __ O __ __   *clue on page 253*

8. __ __ O __ __ I O   *clue on page 261*

```
C G L N P Q R S T V
C         P   R S
C         P   R S
C             R S
              R S
              R S
              R
```

Astronomers Galileo and Copernicus were also both practicing astrologers.

Answers on page 270

SCORE

According to a *LIFE* magazine survey, about 48% of Americans believe in astrology.

WORDS THAT START WITH O

1	O _ Y _	*clue on page 202*
2	O A _ I _	*clue on page 210*
3	O _ E _ A	*clue on page 219*
4	O _ _ _ E Y	*clue on page 227*
5	O A _ _ E A _	*clue on page 236*
6	O _ _ I _ U E	*clue on page 245*
7	O _ E _ I E _ _	*clue on page 253*
8	O _ _ _ E _ _ _ A	*clue on page 261*

```
B C D G H L M N P Q R S T X
B           L M N R     S T
                  R     S T
                        S
```

Haggis, the national dish of Scotland, was originally imported (probably from Scandinavia).

Answers on page 270

SCORE

Traditionally, a knot must have 13 coils to be a true hangman's knot.

EUROPEAN COUNTRIES

1 I _ A _ Y   *clue on page 202*

2 _ _ A _ _ E   *clue on page 211*

3 _ _ E E _ E   *clue on page 219*

4 _ O _ _ A Y   *clue on page 228*

5 E _ _ O _ I A   *clue on page 236*

6 _ E _ _ A _ Y   *clue on page 245*

7 _ O _ _ U _ A _   *clue on page 253*

8 _ U _ E _ _ O U _ _   *clue on page 262*

B C F G L M N P R S T W X
  C   G L M N   R   T
      G L   N   R   T
      G   N   R
             R
             R

Chance that a diamond has passed through Antwerp, Belgium, on its way to market: 80%.

Answers on page 270

SCORE

Nearly 20% of France's territory lies outside of Europe.

THEY'RE JUST GEMS!

1 O _ A _ *clue on page 202*

2 _ U _ Y *clue on page 211*

3 A _ _ E _ *clue on page 219*

4 _ E A _ _ *clue on page 228*

5 _ O _ A _ *clue on page 236*

6 _ I A _ O _ _ *clue on page 245*

7 _ A _ _ _ I _ E *clue on page 253*

8 _ U _ _ U O I _ E *clue on page 262*

B D H L M N P Q R S T Z
B D   L M   P   R S T
           P   R
           P   R
           P   R

Chemist Edmond Fremy created the first synthetic gemstone in 1877. (It was a ruby.)

Answers on page 270

SCORE

Americans buy about $8 billion worth of gems per year.

WORDS THAT START WITH D

1 __ E U __ E   *clue on page 202*

2 __ __ A __ A   *clue on page 211*

3 __ A __ __ I A   *clue on page 219*

4 __ E __ __ I __ Y   *clue on page 228*

5 __ U __ __ E O __   *clue on page 236*

6 __ __ I __ E __ A Y   *clue on page 245*

7 __ I __ __ O __ A __ Y   *clue on page 253*

8 __ __ A __ O __ __ __ Y   *clue on page 262*

```
C D F G H L M N P R S T V W
C D   G   L M N   R
  D       L   N   R
  D           N
  D
  D
  D
  D
```

What's a *digraph*? Two letters that represent a single...

18

Answers on page 271

...sound. (Example: the "ph" at the end of digraph.)

HAWAII

....

1 _ O I   *clue on page 202*

2 _ U _ A   *clue on page 211*

3 _ E I _   *clue on page 219*

4 _ U A U   *clue on page 228*

5 _ A _ A I   *clue on page 236*

6 _ A _ U _ A   *clue on page 245*

7 _ U _ _ I _ _   *clue on page 253*

8 _ A I _ I _ I   *clue on page 262*

....

F G H K L N P R S W
H K L N S
K L N
L

Hawaii's Papahanaumokuakea Marine National Monument is…

Answers on page 271

Answers on page 271

…larger than all of America's National Parks combined.

CARD GAMES

1	__ A __	*clue on page 202*
2	__ O __ E __	*clue on page 211*
3	__ __ I __ __ E	*clue on page 219*
4	__ E A __ __ __	*clue on page 228*
5	__ __ A __ E __	*clue on page 236*
6	__ A __ A __ __ A	*clue on page 245*
7	__ I __ O __ __ __ E	*clue on page 253*
8	__ O __ I __ A I __ E	*clue on page 262*

B C D G H K L N P R S T W
C D   H   L N P R S T
              P R S T
            R S
            R S

The U.S. Playing Card Company sells more than 100 million decks of cards per year.

Answers on page 271

SCORE

World record for the tallest house of cards: 25 feet, 3 $\frac{1}{2}$ inches high.

WORDS THAT START WITH V

1	_ A _ U E	*clue on page 202*
2	_ E _ I _ Y	*clue on page 211*
3	_ O Y E U _	*clue on page 219*
4	_ A _ I _ _ A	*clue on page 228*
5	_ E _ _ E _ _ A	*clue on page 236*
6	_ E _ _ A _ I _	*clue on page 245*
7	_ I _ E Y A _ _	*clue on page 253*
8	_ I _ _ U O _ O	*clue on page 262*

```
B D F G L M N R S T V
  D     L   N R   T V
            N R   T V
              R   T V
              R     V
                    V
                    V
                    V
```

The slash (/) character is also called a *virgule*.

Answers on page 271

What do Marvel and DC Comics have in common? Both have a villain named Hangman.

AT THE ZOO

1 __ E A __ clue on page 203

2 __ A __ A __ clue on page 211

3 __ O __ __ E Y clue on page 220

4 __ O __ I __ __ A clue on page 228

5 __ E O __ A __ __ clue on page 237

6 E __ E __ __ A __ __ clue on page 245

7 __ __ I __ __ A __ __ E E clue on page 254

8 __ I __ __ O __ O __ A __ U __ clue on page 262

B C D G H K L M N P R S T W Z
C   H   L M N P R   T
H   L M N P R
L M   P
P
P

A crocodile's bite is 12 times stronger than a great white shark's.

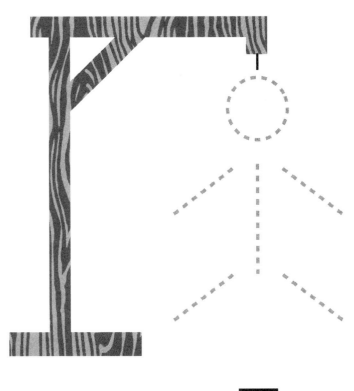

Answers on page 271

SCORE

A group of whales is called a *gam*. A group of moles is called a *labor*.

ONE-NAMED SINGERS

1	_ _ E _		*clue on page 203*
2	E _ Y A		*clue on page 211*
3	_ _ O _ _		*clue on page 220*
4	E _ _ I _		*clue on page 228*
5	_ _ I _ _		*clue on page 237*
6	U _ _ E _		*clue on page 245*
7	_ E Y O _ _ E		*clue on page 254*
8	_ A _ O _ _ A		*clue on page 262*

B C D G H J K L M N R S T V
B C   H   N R S
              N R S
              N
              N

The accent used by many American actors is called a "mid-Atlantic English...

28

Answers on page 271

...accent." Three actors who use it: Kelsey Grammar, David Hyde Pierce, John Lithgow.

GONE FISHIN'

1	_ O _	*clue on page 203*
2	E E _	*clue on page 211*
3	_ A _ _	*clue on page 220*
4	_ _ O U _	*clue on page 228*
5	_ A _ _ I _	*clue on page 237*
6	_ A _ _ I _ _	*clue on page 245*
7	_ I _ A _ _ A	*clue on page 254*
8	_ A _ _ A _ U _ A	*clue on page 262*

```
B C D F H L M N P R S T
B C D   H L   N   R S T
    C             R S T
                  R
                  R
```

Most common fish in the sea: The minnow-size deep-sea bristlemouth.

Answers on page 271

SCORE

The world's oldest fishhook was found in a cave in East Timor. Age: 23,000 years.

BACK TO SCHOOL

1	_ E _	*clue on page 203*
2	_ O O _ _	*clue on page 211*
3	_ U _ E _	*clue on page 220*
4	_ I _ _ E _	*clue on page 228*
5	E _ A _ E _	*clue on page 237*
6	_ A _ _ O _	*clue on page 245*
7	_ A _ _ _ A _ _	*clue on page 254*
8	_ U _ _ _ _ O _	*clue on page 262*

```
B C D H K L N P R S T X
B C     K L N P R S
B C     K L N P R
B             P R
              R
```

Average amount spent by parents on back-to-school clothes: $604.

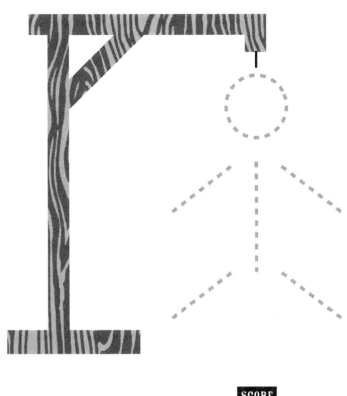

SCORE

Answers on page 271

Highest average salary for U.S. teachers: about $64,000 (CA). Lowest: $35,000 (SD).

WORDS WITH Q IN THEM

1	_ U O _ A	*clue on page 203*
2	U _ I _ U E	*clue on page 211*
3	I _ _ U I _ Y	*clue on page 220*
4	_ E _ U I _ A	*clue on page 228*
5	_ O _ _ U I _ O	*clue on page 237*
6	_ U _ _ E _ _ U E	*clue on page 245*
7	_ _ O _ E _ _ U E	*clue on page 254*
8	_ A _ _ U E _ A _ E	*clue on page 262*

```
B D G L M N Q R S T
    L M N Q R S T
          Q R S T
          Q R S T
          Q
          Q
          Q
          Q
```

American crosswords are about 16% black squares. British crosswords: 50%.

Answers on page 272

SCORE

In Japan, it is customary to give your new landlord a gift of cash equal to 3 months rent.

MUSICAL INSTRUMENTS

1 _ A _ _   *clue on page 203*

2 _ U _ A   *clue on page 211*

3 _ E _ _ O   *clue on page 220*

4 _ _ U _ E   *clue on page 228*

5 _ I A _ O   *clue on page 237*

6 _ I O _ I _   *clue on page 245*

7 _ _ O _ _ O _ E   *clue on page 254*

8 _ A _ O _ _ O _ E   *clue on page 262*

```
B C F H L M N P R S T V X
B     H L   N P R   T
      L   N P     T
      L   N
```

According to experts, the dexterity involved with playing a violin exercises the entire brain.

Answers on page 272

In England, royalty and poachers were traditionally hanged with a silk rope.

GETTING INTO SHAPES

1 _ U _ E   *clue on page 203*

2 _ _ I _ _   *clue on page 212*

3 _ I _ _ _ E   *clue on page 220*

4 _ _ _ E _ E   *clue on page 229*

5 _ _ U A _ E   *clue on page 237*

6 _ E _ _ A _ O _   *clue on page 246*

7 _ _ I A _ _ _ E   *clue on page 254*

8 _ E _ _ A _ _ _ E   *clue on page 263*

```
B C G H L M N P Q R S T
  C G   L   N P   R S T
  C G   L   N P   R S T
  C           N   R
                  R
                  R
```

The U.S. Mint once considered producing donut-shaped coins.

Answers on page 272

In ancient Greece, helmets, legs, and feet were popular shapes for perfume bottles.

WORDS THAT START WITH E

1	E _ O _ Y	*clue on page 203*
2	E _ _ O _	*clue on page 212*
3	E _ _ _ Y	*clue on page 220*
4	E A _ I _ Y	*clue on page 229*
5	E _ I _ _ A	*clue on page 237*
6	E _ A _ _ I _	*clue on page 246*
7	E _ U I _ O _	*clue on page 254*
8	E _ O _ _ I _ _	*clue on page 263*

```
B C G L M N Q R S T W X
B C   L M N   R S T   X
      L   N     S
          N
```

The world's top 10 countries that rank themselves as "unhappy" are all in Eastern Europe.

Answers on page 272

SCORE

If you measured America in pennies laid end-to-end, it would be about $2.5 million wide.

DINING AT A DINER

. . . .

1 _ I E   *clue on page 203*

2 _ O O _   *clue on page 212*

3 _ E _ U   *clue on page 220*

4 _ O O _ _   *clue on page 229*

5 _ U _ A _   *clue on page 237*

6 _ O _ _ E E   *clue on page 246*

7 _ O U _ _ E _   *clue on page 254*

8 _ A I _ _ E _ _   *clue on page 263*

. . . .

B C F G H K M N P R S T W
C F   N   R S T
C   R S T

Ninety percent of diners in the New York region were founded by Greek immigrants.

Answers on page 272

SCORE

First diner: Walter Scott's horse-drawn lunch wagon in Providence, RI (1872).

BOATS

1	_ U _ _	*clue on page 203*
2	_ A _ O E	*clue on page 212*
3	_ A Y A _	*clue on page 220*
4	Y A _ _ _	*clue on page 229*
5	_ _ A _ E _	*clue on page 237*
6	_ _ I _ A _ E	*clue on page 246*
7	_ O _ _ O _ A	*clue on page 254*
8	_ _ _ O O _ E _	*clue on page 263*

```
C D F G H J K L N R S T W
C     G H   K L N R   T
C       H   K   N R
                N
```

Youngest person to sail solo around the world: Australian Jessica Watson, age 16.

Answers on page 272

SCORE

Bad omen? The *Titanic* was never christened.

SOUTH AMERICAN COUNTRIES

1	_ E _ U	*clue on page 203*
2	_ _ I _ E	*clue on page 212*
3	_ _ A _ I _	*clue on page 220*
4	E _ U A _ O _	*clue on page 229*
5	U _ U _ U A Y	*clue on page 237*
6	_ O _ O _ _ I A	*clue on page 246*
7	A _ _ E _ _ I _ A	*clue on page 254*
8	_ E _ E _ U E _ A	*clue on page 263*

```
B C D G H L M N P R T V Z
B C   G   L   N   R     Z
  C       L   N   R
          L       R
                  R
```

When you Google the word "anagram," you're asked, "Did you mean *nag a ram*?"

SCORE

Answers on page 272

Grammatically speaking, an executed person is "hanged," not "hung."

KITCHEN PLUG-INS

1 _ I _ E _   *clue on page 203*

2 _ _ O _ E   *clue on page 212*

3 _ _ E _ _ E _   *clue on page 220*

4 _ O A _ _ E _   *clue on page 229*

5 _ I _ _ O _ A _ E   *clue on page 237*

6 _ I _ _ _ A _ _ E _   *clue on page 246*

7 _ O _ _ E E _ A _ E _   *clue on page 254*

8 _ E _ _ I _ E _ A _ O _   *clue on page 263*

```
B C D F G H K L M N R S T V W X
  C D F   H     M   R S T V W
      F         M   R S T
                    R S T
                    R
                    R
                    R
                    R
                    R
                    R
```

If 10,000 elementary schools turned off their lights for one minute, it could save $81,885.

Answers on page 272

Until 1961 hanging was the only legal form of execution in Canada.

WORDS THAT START WITH N

1 _ O _ A   *clue on page 204*

2 _ E I _ _   *clue on page 212*

3 _ A U _ E A   *clue on page 221*

4 _ O U _ A _   *clue on page 229*

5 _ O _ A _ I _   *clue on page 238*

6 _ Y _ _ _ E _   *clue on page 246*

7 _ E _ _ O _ E _   *clue on page 255*

8 _ O _ _ A _ _ I A   *clue on page 263*

```
C D G H L M N P R S T V W
C   G H   M N     S T
    G     M N       T
          N
          N
          N
          N
          N
```

Most popular town name in Britain: Newtown. (There are more than 150 of them.)

Answers on page 273

"Nintendo" is Japanese for "Leave luck to heaven."

IT'S A BIRD!

1 O _ _ clue on page 204

2 _ O _ I _ clue on page 212

3 O _ I O _ E clue on page 221

4 O _ _ _ I _ _ clue on page 229

5 _ E _ I _ A _ clue on page 238

6 _ _ A _ I _ _ O clue on page 246

7 _ A _ A _ E E _ clue on page 255

8 _ U _ _ I _ _ _ I _ _ clue on page 263

B C D F G H K L M N P R S T W
B C   G H   L M N P R   T
       L M N   R
       L   N   R
            R

Most common bird on Earth: the chicken.

SCORE

Answers on page 273

Avocados can be toxic to birds.

SLANG FOR MONEY

1 _ U _ _ _   *clue on page 204*

2 _ _ A _ _   *clue on page 212*

3 _ _ E A _   *clue on page 221*

4 _ O U _ _   *clue on page 229*

5 _ O O _ A _   *clue on page 238*

6 _ I _ E _ O   *clue on page 246*

7 _ _ A _ _ E _ _   *clue on page 255*

8 _ I _ O _ E O _ _   *clue on page 263*

```
B C D G H K L M N R S
B C D   H K L M N R S
  C D       L M   R S
              M     S
                    S
                    S
```

Of the 180 countries that print their own money, the only one...

Answers on page 273

...that prints all its paper currency in the same size: the U.S.

GREEN __

1	__ E A	*clue on page 204*
2	__ A __ __	*clue on page 212*
3	__ E __ E __	*clue on page 221*
4	__ I __ __ __	*clue on page 229*
5	O __ I O __	*clue on page 238*
6	__ E __ __ E __	*clue on page 246*
7	__ O __ __ E __ __	*clue on page 255*
8	__ A __ __ E __ __	*clue on page 263*

```
B C D G H L N P R S T
  D G   L N P R S T
    D       N P R   T
            N   R   T
```

The word "green" comes from the Latin root for grow.

Answers on page 273

SCORE

Ancient Egyptians painted the floors of their temples green.

TREE'S COMPANY

#	Puzzle	Clue
1	E __ __	*clue on page 204*
2	__ I __ E	*clue on page 212*
3	__ E E __ __	*clue on page 221*
4	__ A __ __ E	*clue on page 229*
5	__ A __ __ U __	*clue on page 238*
6	__ I __ __ O __	*clue on page 246*
7	__ I __ __ O __ Y	*clue on page 255*
8	E U __ A __ Y __ __ U __	*clue on page 264*

```
B C H K L M N P R S T W
  C H   L M N P     T W
  C     L     P       W
        L
        L
        L
```

Tree hugger? Two mature trees supply enough oxygen for a family of four.

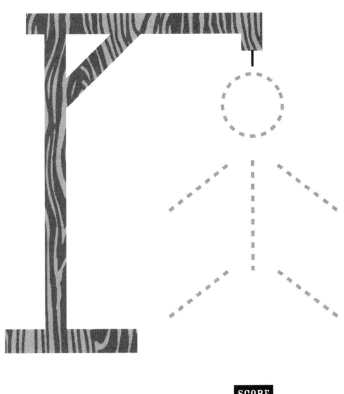

Answers on page 273

SCORE

Put a ring on it: *Dendrochronology* is the science of calculating a tree's age by its rings.

WORDS THAT START WITH A

1 A _ I _ O   *clue on page 204*

2 A _ I O _   *clue on page 212*

3 A _ A _ U _   *clue on page 221*

4 A _ _ A _ _   *clue on page 229*

5 A _ A _ E A   *clue on page 238*

6 A _ A _ O _ E   *clue on page 247*

7 A A _ _ _ A _ _   *clue on page 255*

8 A _ _ E _ _ I _   *clue on page 264*

B C D G H K L M N P R S T V X Z
B   D G   L M N P R S   X

If you're equally skilled with both hands, you're ambidextrous. But if...

Answers on page 273

...you're equally *clumsy* with both hands, you're ambisinistrous.

__ HORSE

#	Puzzle	Clue
1	_ A _ _	*clue on page 204*
2	_ I _ _	*clue on page 213*
3	_ I _ _	*clue on page 221*
4	_ A _ _	*clue on page 230*
5	_ _ A _ Y	*clue on page 238*
6	_ O _ _ Y	*clue on page 247*
7	_ _ O _ _ E _	*clue on page 255*
8	_ O _ _ I _ _	*clue on page 264*

```
B C D F G H K L N P R S T Z
B C     G H K       R   T
  C     G H K       R
  C       H
```

Horses sleep longer in summer than in winter.

Answers on page 273

World's only true wild horse: the Przewalski's horse. It has never been domesticated.

MOUNTAINS

1	E _ _ A	*clue on page 204*
2	_ U _ I	*clue on page 213*
3	_ I _ A I	*clue on page 221*
4	A _ A _ A _	*clue on page 230*
5	E _ E _ E _ _	*clue on page 238*
6	_ _ I _ _ E Y	*clue on page 247*
7	_ A _ _ E _ _ O _ _	*clue on page 255*
8	_ I _ I _ A _ _ A _ O	*clue on page 264*

```
F H J K L M N R S T V W
  H J     M N R S T
          N R   T
          N R   T
          N R   T
            R   T
```

World's highest Internet café: Mt. Everest base camp. (Elevation: 16,600 feet.)

Answers on page 273

SCORE

A stack of the bills destroyed by the U.S. Mint this year would measure 200 miles high.

THE SPACE RACE

1 _ O Y U _   *clue on page 204*

2 A _ O _ _ O   *clue on page 213*

3 _ E _ I _ I   *clue on page 221*

4 _ _ Y _ A _   *clue on page 230*

5 _ _ U _ _ I _   *clue on page 238*

6 _ O Y A _ E _   *clue on page 247*

7 E _ _ E A _ O U _   *clue on page 255*

8 _ I _ _ O _ E _ Y   *clue on page 264*

```
B C D G K L M N P R S T V Z
  D G K L N   P R S   V
      L N       R S   V
                  S
```

While Mt. Everest is Earth's tallest mountain, Mt. Chimborazo is actually closer to the moon.

Answers on page 274

"Jedi" is an official religion with more than 70,000 followers worldwide. (Mostly male.)

MEN IN SMOCKS

1 _ A _ I   *clue on page 204*

2 _ O _ E _   *clue on page 213*

3 _ E _ O I _   *clue on page 221*

4 _ E _ A _ _ E   *clue on page 230*

5 _ A _ I _ _ E   *clue on page 238*

6 _ I _ A _ _ O   *clue on page 247*

7 _ A U _ U I _   *clue on page 255*

8 _ I _ _ E _ A _ _ E _ O   *clue on page 264*

C D G H L M N P R S T Z
C   G   L M N   R S T
C   G   L M N   S
              N   S
              N
              N

The Louvre Museum, built in 1190, was originally designed to be a fortress for King Philip II.

Answers on page 274

SCORE

Early-American colonists made gray paint by boiling blueberries in milk.

WORDS THAT START WITH R

1 _ I O _   *clue on page 204*

2 _ _ I _ O   *clue on page 213*

3 _ E _ I _ A   *clue on page 221*

4 _ O _ O _ O   *clue on page 230*

5 _ A U _ _ _ Y   *clue on page 238*

6 _ E _ _ I _ A   *clue on page 247*

7 _ U _ _ I A _   *clue on page 255*

8 _ E _ E _ A _ E *clue on page 264*

```
C D F G H L N P R T
C   F   H   N   R T
C           N   R
C           N   R
            N   R
                R
                R
                R
```

The language with the fewest sounds: Rotokas (Papua New Guinea), with 11.

Answers on page 274

In Victorian England, mail carriers wore red uniforms and were known as "robins."

BAKERY BUYS

1	_ A _ _	*clue on page 204*
2	_ A _ E _	*clue on page 213*
3	E _ _ A I _	*clue on page 221*
4	_ _ O _ _ I E	*clue on page 230*
5	_ U _ _ A _ E	*clue on page 238*
6	_ O U _ _ _ U _	*clue on page 247*
7	_ A _ O _ E O _	*clue on page 256*
8	_ _ O I _ _ A _ _	*clue on page 264*

```
B C D G H K L N P R S T W
B C   G     L N P R S T
  C         L N   R   T
  C           N   R   T
              N
```

France, a country about the size of Texas, has more than 35,000 bakeries.

Answers on page 274

SCORE

It takes about 400 cacao beans to create 1 lb. of chocolate.

LANGUAGES

1	A _ A _ I _	*clue on page 205*
2	_ _ E _ _ _	*clue on page 213*
3	_ E _ _ A _	*clue on page 222*
4	_ _ I _ E _ E	*clue on page 230*
5	E _ _ _ I _ _	*clue on page 239*
6	I _ A _ I A _	*clue on page 247*
7	_ _ A _ I _ _	*clue on page 256*
8	_ _ A _ I _ I	*clue on page 264*

```
B C F G H L M N P R S T W
  C   G H L   N   R S
  C     H L   N   R S
        H     N     S
        H     N     S
              N
```

Most difficult English sound for foreign students to master: "Th".

Answers on page 274

The German word for hydrogen is *waterstoff*. English translation: "Water stuff."

SCHOOL SUBJECTS

1	A _ _	*clue on page 205*
2	_ A _ I _	*clue on page 213*
3	A _ _ E _ _ A	*clue on page 222*
4	_ I O _ O _ Y	*clue on page 230*
5	_ _ A _ _ A _	*clue on page 239*
6	_ I _ _ O _ Y	*clue on page 247*
7	_ E O _ E _ _ Y	*clue on page 256*
8	_ _ E _ I _ _ _ Y	*clue on page 264*

```
B C G H L M N R S T
B   G H L M   R S T
    G   L M   R   T
    G     M   R   T
            R   T
            R
            R
```

About 2% of American kids are home-schooled.

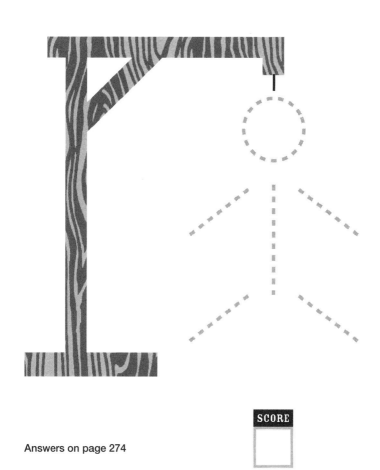

Answers on page 274

SCORE

Muphry's Law: "While correcting somone's grammar, you will make a grammatical error."

WORDS THAT START WITH Y

1 Y E _ I *clue on page 205*

2 Y E _ _ A *clue on page 213*

3 Y O _ E _ *clue on page 222*

4 Y O U _ _ *clue on page 230*

5 Y U _ _ A *clue on page 239*

6 Y A _ _ E _ *clue on page 247*

7 Y E O _ A _ *clue on page 256*

8 Y U _ E _ I _ E *clue on page 264*

```
C D H K L M N R T
C         L M N   T
          M       T
                  T
```

You forget approximately 97% of your dreams.

Answers on page 274

SCORE

Charles Dickens petitioned the British government to have hanging abolished. (He failed.)

MUSICAL GENRES

1 _ O _   *clue on page 205*

2 _ A _   *clue on page 213*

3 _ A _ _   *clue on page 222*

4 _ O _ _   *clue on page 230*

5 _ _ U E _   *clue on page 239*

6 _ E _ _ A E   *clue on page 247*

7 _ A _ Y _ _ O   *clue on page 256*

8 _ O U _ _ _ Y   *clue on page 264*

B C G J K L N P R S T Z
B C G   L   P R S   Z
   C   P R
                  R

The Christmas song "Do You Hear What I Hear?" was written in...

SCORE

Answers on page 274

...1962 as a plea for peace during the Cuban Missile Crisis.

WINE LIST

#		
1	_ O _ _	*clue on page 205*
2	_ _ A _ E _	*clue on page 213*
3	_ E _ _ O _	*clue on page 222*
4	_ _ I A _ _ I	*clue on page 230*
5	_ I E _ _ I _ _	*clue on page 239*
6	_ O _ _ E A U _	*clue on page 247*
7	_ E A U _ O _ A I _	*clue on page 256*
8	_ _ A _ _ O _ _ A Y	*clue on page 264*

```
B C D G H J L M N P R S T X
B C D   H   L   N   R S T
  C         L   N   R   T
            L   N   R   T
                    R
                    R
```

Hiccup! Worldwide, there are more than 10,000 varieties of wine grapes.

SCORE

Answers on page 275

One bottle of wine contains the juice of about 2.8 lb. of grapes.

DOWN UNDER

1 _ I _ _ O   *clue on page 205*

2 _ O A _ A   *clue on page 213*

3 O U _ _ A _ _   *clue on page 222*

4 _ A _ _ A _ O O   *clue on page 230*

5 _ _ A _ Y _ U _   *clue on page 239*

6 _ I _ _ A _ O _ _   *clue on page 247*

7 _ O O _ E _ A _ _   *clue on page 256*

8 _ A _ _ A _ O U _   *clue on page 264*

B	C	D	G	K	L	M	N	P	R	S	T	W
B			G	K	L		N		P	R		T	
B			G	K	L		N					T	
B			G	K	L		N						
B					L								

The slogan "Foster's: Australian for Beer" isn't used in…

84

Answers on page 275

SCORE

…Australia. There, the slogan is "The Amber Nectar."

WORDS THAT START WITH B

1 _ I _ _ O   *clue on page 205*

2 _ _ A _ O   *clue on page 214*

3 _ A _ O O _   *clue on page 222*

4 _ A _ A A _   *clue on page 231*

5 _ A _ O _ U E   *clue on page 239*

6 _ A _ O O _ A   *clue on page 248*

7 _ _ O _ _ A _ _   *clue on page 256*

8 _ A _ _ E _ I _ A   *clue on page 265*

```
B D G H K L N Q R V W Z
B         L N   R     Z
B         L N   R
B               R
B               R
B
B
B
B
```

Teddy Roosevelt gave up boxing, his favorite sport, because…

SCORE

Answers on page 275

..."it seems rather absurd for a president to appear with a black eye."

EXPLORERS

1 _ A _ O _   *clue on page 205*

2 _ _ A _ E   *clue on page 214*

3 _ A _ _ O A   *clue on page 222*

4 _ U _ _ O _   *clue on page 231*

5 _ O _ U _ _ U _   *clue on page 239*

6 _ A _ E _ _ A _   *clue on page 248*

7 _ E _ _ U _ _ I   *clue on page 256*

8 _ _ A _ _ _ A I _   *clue on page 265*

```
B C D G H K L M N P R S T V
B C D   H   L M N P   S
B C         L M N     S
B C         L
    C       L
```

"Hotel India, Mike Oscar Mike!" (That's "Hi, Mom" in the NATO phonetic alphabet.)

SCORE

Answers on page 275

In an 1894 book of games, Hangman was called "Birds, Beasts and Fishes."

OSCAR-WINNING MOVIES

1 __ I __ I   *clue on page 205*

2 __ __ A __ __   *clue on page 214*

3 __ A __ __ Y   *clue on page 222*

4 __ O __ __ Y   *clue on page 231*

5 __ A __ __ __ I   *clue on page 239*

6 __ A __ __ O __   *clue on page 248*

7 __ I __ A __ I __   *clue on page 256*

8 __ A __ A __ __ A __ __ __   *clue on page 265*

```
B C D G H K L M N P R S T
  C   G H       N   R S T
  C   G         N   R   T
  C             N       T
  C                     T
```

Lowest-grossing Best Picture Oscar-winner: *The Hurt Locker*. It earned only $21 million.

SCORE

Answers on page 275

Bob Hope hosted the Academy Awards 18 times, but never won an Oscar.

WORDS THAT START WITH S

1 _ A U _ Y   *clue on page 205*

2 _ O A _ Y   *clue on page 214*

3 _ U E _ E   *clue on page 222*

4 _ _ _ E _ E   *clue on page 231*

5 _ _ _ E _ Y   *clue on page 239*

6 _ U _ _ A _ _ E   *clue on page 248*

7 _ U _ E _ I O _   *clue on page 256*

8 _ _ A _ E _ A _ E   *clue on page 265*

```
B C D H L M N P R S T W
  C   H   M     P R S T
  C             R S T
              S
              S
              S
              S
              S
```

World's toughest tongue twister (according to...

Answers on page 275

...Guinness): "The sixth sick sheik's sixth sheep's sick."

LET US PRAY

1 _ _ A _ E _   *clue on page 205*

2 _ _ U _ _ _   *clue on page 214*

3 _ O _ _ U E   *clue on page 222*

4 _ O _ _ E _ _   *clue on page 231*

5 _ A _ I _ I _ A   *clue on page 239*

6 _ A _ _ E _ _ A _   *clue on page 248*

7 _ O _ A _ _ E _ Y   *clue on page 256*

8 _ Y _ A _ O _ U E   *clue on page 265*

```
B C D G H L M N P Q R S T V
  C   G H L M N     R S T
  C     H L   N     R S T
  C     H     N     S
  C
  C
```

There are about 99,000 public schools in the U.S., and more than 335,000 churches.

Answers on page 275

SCORE

Size of the average congregation in American churches: about 75 people.

POPULAR PASTIMES

1 _ O _ *clue on page 205*

2 _ _ A _ *clue on page 214*

3 _ I _ I _ *clue on page 222*

4 _ I _ _ I _ _ _ _ _ _ _ _ _ _ _ _ _ _ _ _ _ _ _ *clue on page 231*

5 _ O O _ I _ _ _ _ _ _ _ _ _ _ _ _ _ _ _ _ _ _ *clue on page 239*

6 _ E A _ I _ _ _ _ _ _ _ _ _ _ _ _ _ _ _ _ _ _ *clue on page 248*

7 _ I _ _ I A _ _ _ _ _ _ _ _ _ _ _ _ _ _ _ _ *clue on page 256*

8 _ A _ _ E _ I _ _ _ _ _ _ _ _ _ _ _ _ _ _ *clue on page 265*

```
B C D F G H K L N R S T
  C D F G H K L N R S
    D F G     L N R S
        G       N R
        G       N
        G       N
        G
```

First sport to be pictured on the cover of *Sports Illustrated*: baseball.

Answers on page 275

First casino on the Las Vegas Strip: the Pair-O-Dice Club. (It opened in 1931.)

COLLEGES

1 _ U _ E   *clue on page 206*

2 Y A _ E   *clue on page 214*

3 _ O _ _ A _ E   *clue on page 223*

4 O _ E _ _ I _   *clue on page 231*

5 _ O _ U _ _ I A   *clue on page 240*

6 _ _ A _ _ O _ _   *clue on page 248*

7 _ A _ _ _ O U _ _   *clue on page 257*

8 _ _ I _ _ E _ O _   *clue on page 265*

B	C	D	F	G	H	K	L	M	N	P	R	S	T
B	C	D					L	M	N		R		T
	C	D					L		N		R		T
							L		N		R		T
													T

Avg. SAT reading score for the class of 2011: 497 (the lowest since tracking began in 1972).

SCORE

Answers on page 276

Nearly one quarter of all college freshmen need tutoring or remedial help with math.

WORDS WITH F IN THEM

1	_ _ U	*clue on page 206*
2	_ E _ Y	*clue on page 214*
3	_ O _ Y	*clue on page 223*
4	_ O A _ Y	*clue on page 231*
5	_ I E _ _ A	*clue on page 240*
6	_ Y _ _ I _ Y	*clue on page 248*
7	_ O U _ _ A I _	*clue on page 257*
8	_ O O _ _ A _ _ Y	*clue on page 265*

```
D F H L M N R S T X
D F   L M N   S T
  F           T
  F
  F
  F
  F
  F
```

Until the 16th century, the autumn season was commonly called "harvest."

Answers on page 276

SCORE

The London railway once had a special station just for funeral trains.

CARTOON DOGS

1 O _ I E

clue on page 206

2 _ A _ Y

clue on page 214

3 _ _ U _ O

clue on page 223

4 _ _ A _ _

clue on page 231

5 _ A _ _ Y

clue on page 240

6 _ _ O O _ Y

clue on page 248

7 _ _ I _ _ O _ _

clue on page 257

8 _ A _ _ A _ U _ E

clue on page 265

```
C D F K L M N P R S T
  D F   L M N P R S T
  D     L M   P R
  D
  D
```

Dogs have twice as many muscles for moving their ears as people do.

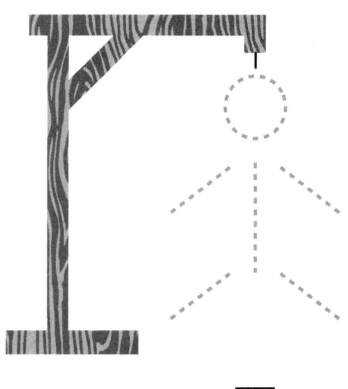

Answers on page 276

SCORE

A German Shepherd guide dog led her blind master the entire 2,100-mile Appalachian Trail.

AFRICAN COUNTRIES

1. _ A _ I   *clue on page 206*

2. _ _ A _ A   *clue on page 214*

3. _ E _ Y A   *clue on page 223*

4. U _ A _ _ A   *clue on page 231*

5. _ O _ O _ _ O   *clue on page 240*

6. E _ _ I O _ I A   *clue on page 248*

7. _ I _ _ A _ _ E   *clue on page 257*

8. _ O _ A _ _ I _ U E   *clue on page 265*

B C D G H K L M N P Q R T W Z
B C   G H   M N   Z
B   M N
              M
              M

Nigeria's version of Cookie Monster is called "Zobi." He's obsessed with yams.

Answers on page 276

Language with the most sounds: the African language !Xóõ. It has 112.

THEY COME IN PAIRS

1	_ O O _ _	*clue on page 206*
2	_ A _ _ _	*clue on page 214*
3	_ _ O E _	*clue on page 223*
4	_ _ I _ _	*clue on page 231*
5	_ _ I E _ _	*clue on page 240*
6	_ _ A _ _ E _	*clue on page 248*
7	E A _ _ I _ _ _	*clue on page 257*
8	_ _ I _ _ O _ _	*clue on page 265*

```
B C G H L N P R S S T W
    G   L N P R S S T
        N   R S S T
            R S S
              S S
              S S
              S S
```

Average weight of twins at birth: about 5.5 lb. each.

Answers on page 276

SCORE

Gemellology is the scientific study of twins.

WORDS THAT START WITH L

1	_ A _ A	*clue on page 206*
2	_ Y _ E	*clue on page 214*
3	_ E _ U _ E	*clue on page 223*
4	_ I _ I _ O	*clue on page 231*
5	_ I A I _ O _	*clue on page 240*
6	_ I _ U E U _	*clue on page 248*
7	_ I _ O _ I _ E	*clue on page 257*
8	_ A _ O _ A _ O _ Y	*clue on page 265*

```
B C D G L M N Q R S T V
B C     L       R
        L       R
        L       R
        L       R
        L
        L
        L
```

The average American family does 8–10 loads of laundry per week.

SCORE

Answers on page 276

Lactose tolerance is a mutation. Lactose *in*tolerance is the original form of the gene.

DOCTOR *WHO*?

1	_ E U _ _	*clue on page 206*
2	_ _ O _ _	*clue on page 215*
3	_ E _ Y _ _	*clue on page 223*
4	_ A _ _ O _	*clue on page 232*
5	_ I _ _ A _ E	*clue on page 240*
6	_ _ I _ A _ O	*clue on page 249*
7	_ O _ I _ _ _ E	*clue on page 257*
8	_ _ _ A _ _ E _ O _ E	*clue on page 266*

```
C D G H J K L N P R S T V W Z
  D G     K L N   R S T V
        K L       S T
          L       S T
          L       S
          L       S
```

So far, 11 actors have played Doctor Who. Longest in the role: Tom Baker (1974–81).

Answers on page 276

SCORE

On average, doctors misdiagnose their patients about 10% of the time.

BLUE __

1	__ E A __ __	*clue on page 206*
2	__ __ O O __	*clue on page 215*
3	__ __ I E __	*clue on page 223*
4	A __ __ E __ __	*clue on page 232*
5	__ __ E E __ E	*clue on page 240*
6	__ O __ __ A __	*clue on page 249*
7	__ I __ __ O __	*clue on page 257*
8	__ __ __ E A __	*clue on page 266*

```
B C D G H J K L N R S T
B C         K L N R S
B             L N R S
                L   S
                    S
                    S
```

Elvis Presley's famous pink Cadillac was originally blue. (He had it repainted.)

SCORE

Answers on page 276

In the ancient Greek language, there was no word for "blue."

BIRDS OF PREY

1	_ A _ _	*clue on page 206*
2	_ I _ E	*clue on page 215*
3	E A _ _ E	*clue on page 223*
4	_ O _ _ O _	*clue on page 232*
5	_ A _ _ O _	*clue on page 240*
6	_ E _ _ _ E _	*clue on page 249*
7	_ U _ _ U _ E	*clue on page 257*
8	_ U _ _ A _ _	*clue on page 266*

B C D F G H K L N R S T V W Z
   C D   K L N R   T   Z
            K L   R   T
              L   R

Seagulls sometimes steal food out of pelicans' beaks.

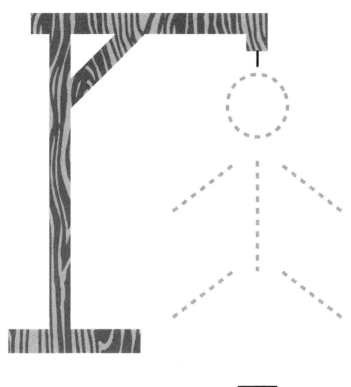

Answers on page 277

SCORE

The earliest-known bird, *Archaeopteryx lithographica*, had a reptilian snout, not a beak.

ON THE CUTTING EDGE

1 _ A _ clue on page 206

2 _ A _ O _ clue on page 215

3 _ _ O _ _ clue on page 223

4 _ A Y O _ E _ clue on page 232

5 _ A _ _ _ E _ clue on page 240

6 _ A _ _ E _ E clue on page 249

7 _ _ I _ E _ _ O clue on page 257

8 _ A _ _ _ _ I _ E clue on page 266

B	C	D	F	H	J	K	L	M	N	R	S	T	W	Z
	C			H		K			N	R	S	T	W	
	C			H						R	S	T		
												T		
												T		
												T		
												T		

The *Official Table of Drops*, first published in 1888, calculated the exact length of rope...

Answers on page 277

...needed for a hanging. (Example: For a person weighing 175 lb, you need 5'11" of rope.)

WORDS WITH X IN THEM

1 _ Y _ _ *clue on page 206*

2 E _ _ O *clue on page 215*

3 E _ O _ Y *clue on page 223*

4 E _ _ _ A *clue on page 232*

5 _ I O U _ *clue on page 240*

6 E _ I _ I _ *clue on page 249*

7 _ E _ A _ O _ *clue on page 257*

8 _ Y _ O _ _ O _ E *clue on page 266*

```
G H L N P R S T X
  H L N P R     X
    L N P       X
              X
              X
              X
              X
              X
```

Olny word in the English language that contains "xyz": hydroxyzine.

Answers on page 277

SCORE

Translated from ancient Phoenician, the word "alphabet" means "ox-house."

PIES

1 A _ _ _ E   *clue on page 206*

2 _ E A _ _ _   *clue on page 215*

3 _ E _ A _   *clue on page 223*

4 _ _ E _ _ Y   *clue on page 232*

5 _ U _ _ A _ _   *clue on page 240*

6 _ U _ _ _ I _   *clue on page 249*

7 _ _ O O _ _ Y   *clue on page 258*

8 _ _ U E _ E _ _ Y   *clue on page 266*

```
B C D F H K L M N P R S T
B C     H   L     N P R S
    C   H   L       P R
    C               P R
                    P R
                    P
```

One in five Americans admits to having eaten an entire pie by themselves.

Answers on page 277

Patron saint of pastry chefs: St. Honoré.

OUTER SPACE

1 _ O _ E _   *clue on page 207*

2 _ O _ _ O _   *clue on page 215*

3 _ A _ A _ Y   *clue on page 224*

4 _ E _ U _ A   *clue on page 232*

5 _ _ A _ E _ _   *clue on page 241*

6 A _ _ E _ O I _   *clue on page 249*

7 U _ I _ E _ _ E   *clue on page 258*

8 A _ _ _ O _ O _ Y   *clue on page 266*

```
B C D G L M N P R S T V X
  C     L M N   R S T
        L M N   R S T
              N   S T
                  S
                  S
```

Cryovolcanoes exist only in outer space. They can be found on icy moons.

Answers on page 277

SCORE

Technically, cosmonaut Sergei Avdeyev time-traveled 0.02 seconds into the future.

NONSENSE!

1 _ O O E Y

clue on page 207

2 _ U _ _ U _

clue on page 215

3 _ A _ O _ E Y

clue on page 224

4 _ O _ _ A _ _

clue on page 232

5 _ O _ _ E _ O _

clue on page 241

6 _ I _ _ E _ I _ _

clue on page 249

7 _ O _ _ Y _ O _ _

clue on page 258

8 _ O _ _ E _ E A _ _ E _ _

clue on page 266

B C D F G H K L M N P R S T W
B C   F G H   L   P R S
B   G H   L   P R S
B   H   R S
        H
        H
        H

In 1955 the NY State Labor Department ruled that "there...

Answers on page 277

...is nothing inherently repulsive about a Van Dyke beard."

IN THE TOOLSHED

1 A _ E   *clue on page 207*

2 _ _ I _ _   *clue on page 215*

3 _ _ A _ _   *clue on page 224*

4 _ E _ E _   *clue on page 232*

5 _ _ I _ E _   *clue on page 241*

6 _ A _ _ E _   *clue on page 249*

7 _ I _ _ A _   *clue on page 258*

8 _ _ _ E _ _ _ I _ E _   *clue on page 266*

C D G H J L M P R S V W X
C D   H   L M   R S V W
C   L M   R S
        L   R
        L   R
        L

Get to work: There are about 800,000 construction companies in the U.S.

Answers on page 277

It is illegal to display a noose in a threatening manner in New York and Connecticut.

WORDS WITH C IN THEM

1 _ O _ Y   *clue on page 207*

2 _ A _ E O   *clue on page 215*

3 _ A _ I A _   *clue on page 224*

4 A _ E _ I _   *clue on page 232*

5 _ I A _ _ O   *clue on page 241*

6 _ _ A _ E _ _ O   *clue on page 249*

7 A _ A _ O _ _ A   *clue on page 258*

8 _ A _ A _ O _ I   *clue on page 266*

```
C D F L M N R S V Z
C   F   M N R
C       M N
C       M N
C         N
C
C
C
```

Q: What is *cryptophasia*? A: The technical name for secret languages created by twins.

Answers on page 277

SCORE

What is *cryptomnesia*? Accidentally plagiarizing someone's work, but believing it's yours.

WORLD RIVERS

1 _ I _ E   *clue on page 207*

2 _ O _ _ O   *clue on page 215*

3 _ _ I _ E   *clue on page 224*

4 _ _ A _ E   *clue on page 232*

5 A _ A _ O _   *clue on page 241*

6 _ A _ U _ E   *clue on page 249*

7 _ _ A _ E _   *clue on page 258*

8 _ I _ _ I _ _ I _ _ I   *clue on page 266*

B	C	D	G	H	K	L	M	N	P	R	S	T	Z
				H			M	N	P		S		
							M	N			S		
								N			S		
								N			S		
								N			S		

"Apple" and "gold" are among the oldest English words. How old? Around 14,000 years.

130

Answers on page 278

SCORE

There is a mailbox on the Great Barrier Reef.

SHALL WE DANCE?

1	_ I _	clue on page 207
2	_ O _ A	clue on page 215
3	_ A _ _ A	clue on page 224
4	_ A _ _ O	clue on page 232
5	_ I _ _ O	clue on page 241
6	_ O _ _ A	clue on page 249
7	_ I _ U E _	clue on page 258
8	_ _ A _ _ E _ _ O _	clue on page 266

```
B C G H J K L M N P R S T
B   G H     L M N   R S T
            L M N       T
```

Capoeira is a Brazilian martial art that includes music, singing, and dance.

Answers on page 278

SCORE

The character and song "Rudolph the Red-Nosed Reindeer" are trademarked.

WORDS WITH P IN THEM

1	_ A _ I O	clue on page 207
2	_ _ I _ Y	clue on page 216
3	U _ O _ I A	clue on page 224
4	_ I _ U A _ _	clue on page 233
5	_ _ E _ I U _	clue on page 241
6	O _ I _ I O _	clue on page 250
7	_ E _ I _ _ U _ A	clue on page 258
8	_ O _ _ U _ O _ I A	clue on page 267

```
C L M N P Q R S T V
C   M N P     R   T
      N P     R   T
      N P
      N P
      N P
        P
        P
```

Most-looked-up word at Merriam-Webster.com: pretentious.

Answers on page 278

March 17 should be Maewyn Succat Day. That was Saint Patrick's real name.

ASIAN COUNTRIES

1 _ A O _   *clue on page 207*

2 _ _ I _ A   *clue on page 216*

3 _ A _ A _   *clue on page 224*

4 _ E _ A _   *clue on page 233*

5 _ A I _ A _   *clue on page 241*

6 _ I E _ _ A _   *clue on page 250*

7 _ A _ _ O _ I A   *clue on page 258*

8 _ _ A I _ A _ _   *clue on page 267*

```
B C D H J L M N P S T V W
  C D H   L M N P   T
        L   N     T
            N
            N
            N
```

40% of all printed material sold in Japan is manga.

Answers on page 278

SCORE

Bangkok, the name of the capital city of Thailand, means "wild plum village"

HATS

1	__ E __	*clue on page 207*
2	__ E __ __ Y	*clue on page 216*
3	__ E A __ I E	*clue on page 224*
4	__ O __ __ E __	*clue on page 233*
5	__ E __ __ E __	*clue on page 241*
6	__ I __ __ __ O __	*clue on page 250*
7	__ I __ __ __ __ A __	*clue on page 258*
8	__ O __ __ __ E __ O	*clue on page 267*

B C D F G H L M N P R S T X Z
B   H L M N P R   T
B   L   N   R   T
B   N
B

In 18th-century Paris, it was fashionable to attach small lightning rods to women's hats.

Answers on page 278

In religious imagery, the glow around the head of a saint is a *gloriole*.

BOARD GAMES

1 _ _ U E   *clue on page 207*

2 _ I _ _   *clue on page 216*

3 _ _ E _ _ E _ _   *clue on page 224*

4 _ O _ O _ O _ Y   *clue on page 233*

5 _ _ _ A _ _ _ E   *clue on page 241*

6 _ A _ _ _ E E _ I   *clue on page 250*

7 _ A _ _ _ A _ _ O _   *clue on page 258*

8 _ A _ _ _ E _ _ I _   *clue on page 267*

```
B C G H K L M N P R S T
B C   H K L M N P R S T
B C   H K L M   P R S
B C       L       R S
  C               S
  C
```

Original Monopoly tokens included a purse, a rocking horse, and a lantern.

140

Answers on page 278

SCORE

Scrabble creator Alfred Butts limited the number of "S" tiles to make the game harder.

THE V-8 EIGHT

1. _ E E _ _ *clue on page 207*
2. _ E _ E _ Y *clue on page 216*
3. _ A _ _ O _ _ *clue on page 224*
4. _ E _ _ U _ E *clue on page 233*
5. _ A _ _ _ E Y *clue on page 241*
6. _ _ I _ A _ _ *clue on page 250*
7. _ O _ A _ O E _ *clue on page 258*
8. _ A _ E _ _ _ E _ _ *clue on page 267*

B	C	H	L	M	N	P	R	S	T	W
	C		L			P	R	S	T	
	C		L				R	S	T	
	C						R	S	T	
	C						R	S	T	
							R	S	T	
								S	T	

Oh, yeah! Kool-Aid was originally called "Fruit Smack."

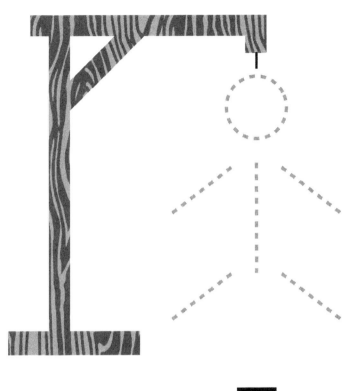

 SCORE

Answers on page 278

Procter & Gamble chose the name "Pringles" from a phone book.

AT THE CIRCUS

1 _ I O _ _   clue on page 207

2 _ _ O _ _ _   clue on page 216

3 _ U _ _ _ E _   clue on page 224

4 _ _ A _ E _ E   clue on page 233

5 A _ _ O _ A _ _   clue on page 241

6 U _ I _ Y _ _ E   clue on page 250

7 _ I _ _ _ _ O _ E   clue on page 258

8 _ I _ _ _ A _ _ E _   clue on page 267

```
B C G H J L M N P R S T W Z
  C G     L   N P R S T
  C G     L   N   R S T
  C G     L   N   R S T
                  R   T
                  R
```

Horses cannot breathe through their mouths.

Answers on page 278

Did he magically change it? Harry Houdini's real name was Ehrich Weiss.

PASTA

1	_ I _ I	*clue on page 208*
2	_ E _ _ E	*clue on page 216*
3	_ A _ I O _ I	*clue on page 225*
4	_ A _ A _ _ A	*clue on page 233*
5	_ I _ A _ O _ I	*clue on page 242*
6	_ E _ _ U _ I _ E	*clue on page 250*
7	_ _ A _ _ E _ _ I	*clue on page 259*
8	_ A _ I _ O _ _ I	*clue on page 267*

```
C F G H L M N P R S T V Z
C   G   L   N P R S T
    G       N       T
            N       T
            N       T
            N       T
                    T
                    T
```

Huh? The English word "dinner" comes from the French word for breakfast.

Answers on page 279

The "you deserve a break today" McDonald's jingle was written by Barry Manilow.

WORDS WITH M IN THEM

1 A _ O _ A   *clue on page 208*

2 _ U _ _ O   *clue on page 216*

3 _ O _ I E   *clue on page 225*

4 _ _ _ A _   *clue on page 233*

5 _ A _ A _ I   *clue on page 242*

6 _ O _ _ U _ A   *clue on page 250*

7 _ _ U _ A _ I   *clue on page 259*

8 _ Y _ A _ I _ E   *clue on page 267*

```
B C D F G L M N R S T X
    L M N R S T
        M   R S
        M
        M
        M
        M
        M
```

A farm in Bjurholm, Sweden, makes moose cheese. Price: $500 per lb.

 SCORE

Answers on page 279

Safety first? The most commonly earned Boy Scout merit badge: First Aid.

PARDON MY FRENCH

1 A _ I E U   clue on page 208

2 _ E _ U _   clue on page 216

3 _ O U _ E   clue on page 225

4 E _ _ O _ E   clue on page 233

5 _ E _ O I _   clue on page 242

6 _ _ A _ E A U   clue on page 250

7 E _ _ A _ _ O _   clue on page 259

8 _ O _ _ I E _ _ E   clue on page 267

```
B C D G H M N R S T
  C D G   M N R   T
  C   G       R   T
  C           R
  C           R
```

What do Tina Turner, Brad Pitt, and Elton John have in common? They…

150

Answers on page 279

...all own homes in France.

TIMBER TIME

1	O A __	*clue on page 208*
2	A __ __ E __	*clue on page 216*
3	__ I __ __ __	*clue on page 225*
4	__ E __ A __	*clue on page 233*
5	__ __ __ U __ E	*clue on page 242*
6	__ O __ __ A __	*clue on page 250*
7	__ E __ __ O O __	*clue on page 259*
8	__ A __ __ __ O __ __	*clue on page 267*

B C D H K L N P R S T W
C D H   N P R S   W
C D H   P R
      P R
       R
       R

Most of a tree's roots are shallow. The majority are in the top 12 inches of soil.

SCORE

Answers on page 279

Almost all trees produce flowers.

WORDS WITH Z IN THEM

1 _ I _   *clue on page 208*

2 _ O _ O   *clue on page 216*

3 _ A _ Y   *clue on page 225*

4 O _ O _ E   *clue on page 233*

5 E _ _ A _ _   *clue on page 242*

6 _ _ A _ _ A   *clue on page 250*

7 _ I _ _ A _ _   *clue on page 259*

8 _ E _ _ E _ _ O U _   *clue on page 267*

```
B D L N P R S T V Z Z
    N P R S T   Z Z
    N     S     Z Z
              Z Z
              Z Z
                Z
```

NY Times crossword puzzles get progressively harder from Mon. (easy) to Sat. (hard).

SCORE

Answers on page 279

First use of the word "zoo": the London Zoo—short for London Zoological Gardens (1829).

BROADWAY MUSICALS

1 _ A _ _ — *clue on page 208*

2 _ E _ _ — *clue on page 216*

3 _ A I _ — *clue on page 225*

4 A _ _ I E — *clue on page 233*

5 _ I _ _ E _ — *clue on page 242*

6 _ A _ A _ E _ — *clue on page 250*

7 _ A _ E _ O _ — *clue on page 259*

8 _ _ I _ A _ O O _ — *clue on page 267*

```
B C D G H K L M N R S T
B C             M N R S T
  C               N R   T
                  N R   T
                        T
```

The Christmas song "Silver Bells" was originally called "Tinkle Bells," until...

Answers on page 279

…composer Jay Livingston's wife told him that "tinkle" had another meaning.

HOUSE STYLES

		clue
1	_ A _ I _	*clue on page 208*
2	I _ _ O O	*clue on page 217*
3	_ _ A _ E _	*clue on page 225*
4	_ E E _ E E	*clue on page 234*
5	_ O _ _ A _ E	*clue on page 242*
6	_ A _ _ I O _	*clue on page 251*
7	_ U _ _ A _ O _	*clue on page 259*
8	_ O _ _ _ O U _ E	*clue on page 268*

```
B C G H L M N P S T W
B C G H L   N   S T W
  C G   L   N     T
            N     T
            N     T
```

Historically, feng shui was used to place buildings in harmony with their surroundings.

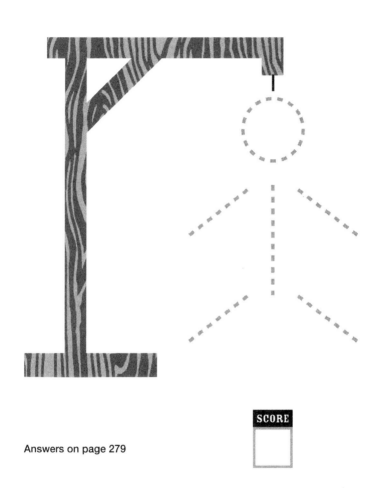

Answers on page 279

SCORE

First prefabricated house: The Aladdin Company began selling house "kits" by mail in 1906.

WORDS WITH J IN THEM

1 _ A _ A   *clue on page 208*

2 _ U _ O   *clue on page 217*

3 _ _ O _ _   *clue on page 225*

4 _ U I _ Y   *clue on page 234*

5 _ A _ U A _   *clue on page 242*

6 _ A _ A _ A _   *clue on page 251*

7 _ A _ E _ _ Y   *clue on page 259*

8 _ A _ _ _ E A _ E _   *clue on page 268*

B C D F G J K M P R S T V W
D   J   M   R S
        J   R
        J   R
        J
        J
        J
        J

Jacuzzi is a brand name. Jacuzzi products (besides hot tubs): toilets and mattresses.

Answers on page 279

First celebrity to appear on *Sesame Street*: James Earl Jones.

IN THE TOY BOX

1 _ O _ — *clue on page 208*

2 _ E _ O _ — *clue on page 217*

3 _ A _ _ _ — *clue on page 225*

4 _ _ O _ _ _ — *clue on page 234*

5 _ A _ _ I E — *clue on page 242*

6 _ _ I _ _ Y — *clue on page 251*

7 _ A _ _ _ E _ — *clue on page 259*

8 _ I _ _ E _ _ O Y _ — *clue on page 268*

B	C	G	J	K	L	M	N	P	R	S	T
B	C			K	L		N		R	S	T
B				K	L				R	S	T
B				K	L					S	
										S	
										S	

Every Halloween, Americans spend $300 million on pet costumes.

Answers on page 280

SCORE

Most common name in nursery rhymes: Jack.

WINE-Y WORDS

1	O A _ Y	*clue on page 208*
2	_ _ I _ _	*clue on page 217*
3	_ E _ _ O _	*clue on page 225*
4	_ _ O O _ _	*clue on page 234*
5	I _ _ E _ _ E	*clue on page 242*
6	_ I _ U A _ _	*clue on page 251*
7	_ E _ _ E _ Y	*clue on page 259*
8	_ U _ _ - _ O _ I E _	*clue on page 268*

```
B C D F H K L M N P Q R S T V W
    D         L M N P       S T V
              L   N         S T
              L             T
              L
```

According to British researchers, eating bacon helps cure a hangover.

Answers on page 280

SCORE

The world's oldest known bottle of wine dates back to 325 A.D.

THE WILD, WILD WEST

1	__ A __ __ __	*clue on page 208*
2	__ __ U __ __	*clue on page 217*
3	__ A __ __ __ E	*clue on page 225*
4	__ O __ __ A __	*clue on page 234*
5	O U __ __ A __	*clue on page 242*
6	__ U __ __ A __ O O	*clue on page 251*
7	__ U __ __ __ O U __ E	*clue on page 259*
8	__ U __ __ __ E __ E E __	*clue on page 268*

```
B C D H K L M N P R S T W
B C   H K L   N   R S T W
B C       L       R S T
  C       L       R   T
                  R
```

Infamous "hanging judge" Roy Bean sentenced only two men to hang...and one escaped.

Answers on page 280

SCORE

In 1988 George H. W. Bush briefly considered naming Clint Eastwood as his running mate.

WORDS WITH W IN THEM

1 A _ _ Y   *clue on page 208*

2 _ E O _   *clue on page 217*

3 _ O _ _ Y   *clue on page 225*

4 _ A _ _ _   *clue on page 234*

5 _ E A _ O _   *clue on page 242*

6 _ _ Y _ O O _   *clue on page 251*

7 _ U _ E _ A _ _   *clue on page 259*

8 _ _ A _ A _ A _   *clue on page 268*

```
C D G H K L M P R S T W Z
  D       L M   R     W
  D       L M         W
          L           W
                      W
                      W
                      W
                      W
```

What do MOW, SIS, and SWIMS have in common? (Turn this page upside down.)

Answers on page 280

Worldwide, houses in English-speaking countries have the most rooms.

SCARY CREATURES

1 _ A _ _   *clue on page 209*

2 _ _ O _ _   *clue on page 217*

3 _ _ O U _   *clue on page 226*

4 _ I _ _ _   *clue on page 234*

5 _ O _ _ I E   *clue on page 243*

6 _ O _ _ _ E _   *clue on page 251*

7 _ A _ _ I _ E   *clue on page 260*

8 _ A _ _ O Y _ E   *clue on page 268*

B C G H L M N P R S T V W Z
B   G H L M   R S T
    G H   M   R S T
    G   T

What is *teratophobia*? The fear of monsters.

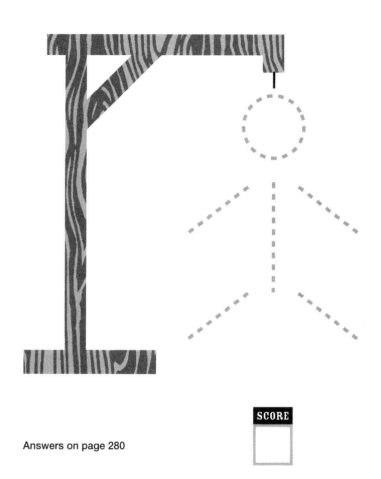

SCORE

Answers on page 280

Highest-grossing Halloween movie of all time: *Jaws* (1975). It pulled in $842 million.

BOGUS

1	_ U _	*clue on page 209*
2	_ A _ E	*clue on page 217*
3	_ A _ _ E	*clue on page 226*
4	_ I _ _ Y	*clue on page 234*
5	_ _ O _ Y	*clue on page 243*
6	_ _ E U _ O	*clue on page 251*
7	_ _ E _ E _ _	*clue on page 260*
8	_ O U _ _ E _ _ E I _	*clue on page 268*

```
B C D F H K L M N P R S T
    D F H       N P R S T
      F         N P   S T
      F
```

Leonard Maltin's complete review of the 1948 film *Isn't It Romantic*?: "No."

Answers on page 280

SCORE

The European Parliament leaves seat number 666 vacant.

WORDS WITH U IN THEM

1. **_ U _ _**   *clue on page 209*

2. **A _ U _ E**   *clue on page 217*

3. **_ A U _ A**   *clue on page 226*

4. **_ O U _ A _**   *clue on page 234*

5. **_ O U _ O _**   *clue on page 243*

6. **U _ _ I _ E**   *clue on page 251*

7. **_ E _ O _ U _**   *clue on page 260*

8. **_ U _ _ I _ _ E _**   *clue on page 268*

```
B C D F G H M N P R Z
  C D   G   M N P R Z
  C         M N   R Z
                  R
                  R
```

The word "uptown" was in use before the word "downtown" was.

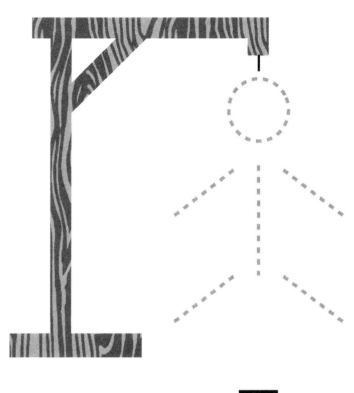

SCORE

Answers on page 280

Model for the original "Uncle Sam" poster: the painter, James Montgomery Flagg.

A HORSE, OF COURSE

1 _ A Y   *clue on page 209*

2 _ A I _ _   *clue on page 217*

3 _ U _ _ A _ _   *clue on page 226*

4 _ I E _ A _ _   *clue on page 234*

5 _ _ E _ _ _ U _   *clue on page 243*

6 _ A _ O _ I _ O   *clue on page 251*

7 A _ _ A _ O O _ A   *clue on page 260*

8 _ _ Y _ E _ _ A _ E   *clue on page 268*

```
B C D G H L M N P S T
B C D     L M N P S T
    D     L   N P S T
          L   N P S T
          L     P
```

The orange stitching on the back pockets of Levi's jeans is called…

SCORE

Answers on page 280

...arcuate. During World War II rationing, it was painted on.

WHERE THE WHITE THINGS ARE

1 _ I _ _ _   *clue on page 209*

2 _ A _ _ _   *clue on page 217*

3 _ U _ A _   *clue on page 226*

4 _ _ O U _   *clue on page 234*

5 I _ O _ Y   *clue on page 243*

6 _ A _ E _   *clue on page 251*

7 I _ E _ E _ _   *clue on page 260*

8 U _ I _ O _ _   *clue on page 268*

```
B C F G K L M N P R S T V
  C   G   L   N P R S
          L       R
                  R
                  R
                  R
```

The ancient Greeks wore white to bed to ensure pleasant dreams.

Answers on page 281

Makes sense: Mauna Kea means "white mountain" in Hawaiian.

THINGS FROM CHINA

1 _ I _ E
clue on page 209

2 _ A _ _ O O
clue on page 217

3 _ _ A _ O _
clue on page 226

4 _ O _ _ A _ _
clue on page 234

5 _ O O _ _ E _
clue on page 243

6 _ U _ _ O _ _ E _
clue on page 251

7 _ _ O _ _ _ I _ _ _
clue on page 260

8 A _ U _ U _ _ _ U _ E
clue on page 268

B C D G H K L M N P R S T W
B C D G   M N P R S T
  C D   N P R S
  C   N P R S
  C   S
  C

China consumes twice as much steel as the United States, Europe, and Japan combined.

Answers on page 281

Around 95% of all software used in China is pirated software.

THINGS THAT ARE GREEN

1 __ A __ E
clue on page 209

2 __ I __ __
clue on page 218

3 A __ __ A E
clue on page 226

4 __ __ A __ __
clue on page 235

5 __ E __ __ I __
clue on page 243

6 __ O __ __ A __
clue on page 252

7 __ I __ __ __ E __
clue on page 260

8 __ __ O __ __ O __ I
clue on page 269

B C D G J K L M N P R S T
C D G   K L M   R S T
C   L   R S
        L   R
        L

How many Boy Scouts make it to the top rank of Eagle Scout? 5%.

Answers on page 281

SCORE

Japanese folklore has a monster called *akaname*, or "filth-eater." (It licks bathroom mildew.)

WORDS WITH H IN THEM

1 _ E _   *clue on page 209*

2 _ I _ _   *clue on page 218*

3 _ A _ _ O _   *clue on page 226*

4 _ U _ _ U _   *clue on page 235*

5 _ _ A _ A _ E   *clue on page 243*

6 _ E _ I _ _ _   *clue on page 252*

7 _ E A _ _ E _ _   *clue on page 260*

8 _ Y _ _ _ O _ Y   *clue on page 269*

B	C	D	F	G	H	L	M	N	P	R	S	T	X
B		D		G	H	L	M				S	T	
B					H	L					S		
					H						S		
					H								
					H								
					H								
					H								

Remember this: *Hyperthymesia* is a rare condition in which…

Answers on page 281

SCORE

...a person can remember almost everything they've ever experienced.

TRADEMARKS

1 _ Y _ E _   clue on page 209

2 _ _ O _ O _   clue on page 218

3 _ U _ I _ E   clue on page 226

4 _ I _ _ E _   clue on page 235

5 _ O _ _ I _ A   clue on page 243

6 _ A _ A _ _ O   clue on page 252

7 _ O _ _ I _ _ E   clue on page 260

8 _ A _ E _ I _ E   clue on page 269

```
B C D F L M N P R S T V W X
  C     L   N P R S T     X
  C     L     P R S       X
  C     L
  C
```

What do linoleum, kerosene, and jungle gym have...

SCORE

Answers on page 281

...in common? All were once trademarked brand names.

WORDS WITH TWO Y's

1 _ _ Y _ O Y *clue on page 209*

2 _ A Y _ A Y *clue on page 218*

3 _ _ Y _ A _ Y *clue on page 226*

4 A _ Y _ O _ Y *clue on page 235*

5 _ _ A Y _ O Y *clue on page 243*

6 _ A Y _ E _ _ Y *clue on page 252*

7 _ U _ Y _ O _ Y *clue on page 260*

8 E _ E _ Y _ A Y *clue on page 269*

B	C	D	F	L	M	N	P	R	S	V	W
B		D		L				R			
B		D		L				R			
B								R			
B											
B											
B											
B											

Monopoly's "Community Chest" was named after the organization now called United Way.

Answers on page 281

SCORE

In Spanish-speaking countries, *Tuesday* the 13th is considered unlucky.

JAIL, TO A JAILBIRD

1	_ _ I _	*clue on page 209*
2	_ _ I _ _	*clue on page 218*
3	_ O I _ _	*clue on page 226*
4	_ O _ E Y	*clue on page 235*
5	_ O O _ E _	*clue on page 243*
6	_ O _ _ U _	*clue on page 252*
7	_ _ A _ _ E _	*clue on page 260*
8	_ O O _ E _ O _	*clue on page 269*

```
C G H J K L M N P R S T W
C       K L M N P R S T
C       K L       R S
        L
```

In 1571 a huge gallows was erected in the village of Tyburn, outside London. Called...

SCORE

Answers on page 281

...the "Tyburn Tree," it was designed to hang up to 24 prisoners at once.

WORDS THAT START WITH I

1	I _ E A	clue on page 209
2	I _ _ E _	clue on page 218
3	I _ _ A _ A	clue on page 226
4	I _ _ A _ _	clue on page 235
5	I _ _ _ U _ E	clue on page 243
6	I _ _ E _ _ A _	clue on page 252
7	I _ _ U _ _ E _ _	clue on page 260
8	I _ _ _ E _ _ O _	clue on page 269

```
C D G L M N P R S T V X
  D   L   N P R S T
  D   L   N   R   T
  D   L   N       T
  D       N
          N
          N
```

In 2009 Iowa changed the Dept. of Elder Affairs (DEA) to the Dept. on Aging, or DOA.

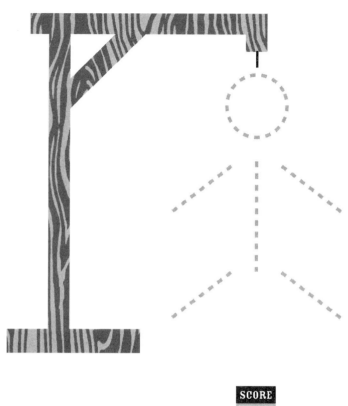

Answers on page 281

SCORE

78.1% of Americans surveyed would like their doctor to greet them with a handshake.

U.S. PLACES WITH INDIAN NAMES

1 _ I A _ I   *clue on page 210*

2 _ A _ I _ U   *clue on page 218*

3 _ O _ E _ A   *clue on page 227*

4 _ O _ O _ E _   *clue on page 235*

5 _ A _ _ _ E _   *clue on page 244*

6 _ U _ _ E _ E E   *clue on page 252*

7 _ A _ _ U _ _ E _   *clue on page 261*

8 _ E _ _ A _ O _ A   *clue on page 269*

```
B C G H K L M N P S T Z
B C   H K L M N P S T
  C     K   M N     T
        K     N     T
              N     T
```

The unfortunate airport code of Sioux City Gateway Airport: SUX.

Answers on page 282

Technically, it's not a "high-wire act" unless the wire is at least 20 feet high.

WORDS WITH K IN THEM

1	_ I _ I	*clue on page 210*
2	_ A _ _ A	*clue on page 218*
3	_ U _ _ Y	*clue on page 227*
4	_ E A _ _ I _	*clue on page 235*
5	_ A _ _ _ O _	*clue on page 244*
6	_ _ O _ _ E _	*clue on page 252*
7	_ I _ _ Y _ A _ _	*clue on page 261*
8	_ I _ _ _ U E A _	*clue on page 269*

```
B C G J K L M N P Q R S T W
B C G   K L   N P   R S T
B       K       P
        K       P
        K
        K
        K
        K
```

The Japanese word *takai* can mean both "tall" and "expensive."

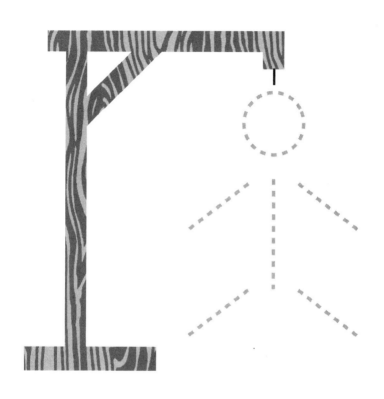

Answers on page 282

Language with the fewest words: Taki-Taki (Surinam). It has only 340 words.

THINGS FROM JAPAN

1	_ U _ O	*clue on page 210*
2	_ U _ _ I	*clue on page 218*
3	_ A I _ U	*clue on page 227*
4	_ E I _ _ A	*clue on page 235*
5	_ I _ O _ O	*clue on page 244*
6	_ A _ A O _ E	*clue on page 252*
7	O _ I _ A _ I	*clue on page 261*
8	_ A _ U _ A I	*clue on page 269*

```
G H K M N R S
G H K M   R S
  H K M   R S
    K M     S
            S
```

In Japanese homes, the toilet is never located in the same room as the bathtub.

Answers on page 282

SCORE

More than half of all single adults in Japan live with their parents.

FIVE-VOWEL WORDS

1 _ E _ U O I A   *clue on page 210*

2 _ I A _ O _ U E   *clue on page 218*

3 _ A _ E _ I O U _   *clue on page 227*

4 _ O U _ E _ A I _   *clue on page 235*

5 _ _ E U _ O _ I A   *clue on page 244*

6 E _ _ A U _ _ I O _   *clue on page 252*

7 _ A _ _ O U _ I _ E   *clue on page 261*

8 _ A U _ I _ _ O _ E _   *clue on page 269*

B C D F G H L M N P Q R S T W X
C D F   H L M N   R S T
    L M N   S T
      N   S

Only U.S. city whose name is all vowels: Aiea, HI.

SCORE

Answers on page 282

Check it yourself: The bottom row of a QWERTY keyboard has no vowels.

WORD LIST 1: **THE PLANETS**

1 An anagram of ARMS.

WORD LIST 2: **WORDS THAT START WITH G**

1 Can U find a spiritual mentor with his rug on backwards?

WORD LIST 3: **WAYS TO SAY HI AND BYE**

1 One of those solo letters works here.

WORD LIST 4: **WORDS THAT START WITH T**

1 Miso soup ingredient.

WORD LIST 5: **STAR SIGNS**

1 Rearrange these letters for a bullfight cry.

WORD LIST 6: **WORDS THAT START WITH O**

1 X marks the (last) spot.

WORD LIST 7: **EUROPEAN COUNTRIES**

1 Gucci's home, and birthplace of the piano.

WORD LIST 8: **THEY'RE JUST GEMS!**

1 You might find this gem in Alpo, but mixed up a little.

WORD LIST 9: **WORDS THAT START WITH D**

1 Take a letter out of "deduce" and you've lost one but gained "two."

WORD LIST 10: **HAWAII**

1 Polynesian finger food.

WORD LIST 11: **CARD GAMES**

1 Word that can precede cry, horse, chest, or dance.

WORD LIST 12: **WORDS THAT START WITH V**

1 Finding this a bit fuzzy? Try the G.

WORD LIST 13: AT THE ZOO
1 Fozzie is one.

WORD LIST 14: ONE-NAMED SINGERS
1 What would a dog-catcher be without this? Just a strange dog-cat.

WORD LIST 15: GONE FISHIN'
1 Fish often used in fish sticks.

WORD LIST 16: BACK TO SCHOOL
1 Where you might find ink—or an oink.

WORD LIST 17: WORDS WITH Q IN THEM
1 Trouble placing the Q?:-)

WORD LIST 18: MUSICAL INSTRUMENTS
1 It has more than 40 strings.

WORD LIST 19: GETTING INTO SHAPES
1 The B fits here.

WORD LIST 20: WORDS THAT START WITH E
1 Take away first letter and what's left is like a witch's fingers.

WORD LIST 21: DINING AT A DINER
1 Could be apple or blueberry.

WORD LIST 22: BOATS
1 The J fits in this Hong Kong harbor sight.

WORD LIST 23: SOUTH AMERICAN COUNTRIES
1 Feel free to take a P here.

WORD LIST 24: KITCHEN PLUG-INS
1 The X works here.

WORD LIST 25: **WORDS THAT START WITH N**

1 The V fits in this heavenly sight.

WORD LIST 26: **IT'S A BIRD!**

1 Bird that give a hoot.

WORD LIST 27: **MONEY SLANG**

1 Put a C in the middle and an S on the end.

WORD LIST 28: **GREEN ___**

1 It also precedes rose, bag, or time.

WORD LIST 29: **TREE'S COMPANY**

1 *A Nightmare on ___ Street*

WORD LIST 30: **WORDS THAT START WITH A**

1 Chum, in Chihuahua.

WORD LIST 31: **___ HORSE**

1 Like some secrets and chocolates.

WORD LIST 32: **MOUNTAINS**

1 Read backwards, it's what you kick in to get a pot going.

WORD LIST 33: **THE SPACE RACE**

1 Z works here.

WORD LIST 34: **MEN IN SMOCKS**

1 Think melting watches.

WORD LIST 35: **WORDS THAT START WITH R**

1 No help here—it's a gimme!

WORD LIST 36: **BAKERY BUYS**

1 Like sour ball candies.

WORD LIST 37: **LANGUAGES**

1 "Algebra" and "hashish" come from this language.

WORD LIST 38: **SCHOOL SUBJECTS**

1 Sketchy word for a mixed-up RAT.

WORD LIST 39: **WORDS THAT START WITH Y**

1 Himalayan critter of legend, or Nepal's ___ Airlines.

WORD LIST 40: **MUSICAL GENRES**

1 A B fits here.

WORD LIST 41: **WINE LIST**

1 Starts with P.

WORD LIST 42: **DOWN UNDER**

1 Rearrange DOING for this Aussie critter.

WORD LIST 43: **WORDS THAT START WITH B**

1 The G goes here.

WORD LIST 44: **EXPLORERS**

1 First three letters are a synonym for taxi.

WORD LIST 45: **OSCAR-WINNING MOVIES**

1 The first three letters spell a word for a singer's job.

WORD LIST 46: **WORDS THAT START WITH S**

1 Like a pert wench.

WORD LIST 47: **LET US PRAY**

1 This word stars with a synonym for "fellow."

WORD LIST 48: **POPULAR PASTIMES**

1 Mark Twain called it "a good walk ruined."

WORD LIST 49: COLLEGES
1 The K works here.

WORD LIST 50: WORDS WITH F IN THEM
1 Something you don't want to catch.

WORD LIST 51: CARTOON DOGS
1 Garfield's pal and sometime victim.

WORD LIST 52: AFRICAN COUNTRIES
1 Turn the MAIL around for this one.

WORD LIST 53: THEY COME IN PAIRS
1 Starts with B.

WORD LIST 54: WORDS THAT START WITH L
1 Put these four letters before "-tory" to get a throne room for Uncle John!

WORD LIST 55: DOCTOR WHO?
1 Think *Green Eggs and Ham*.

WORD LIST 56: BLUE ___
1 The J goes here.

WORD LIST 57: BIRDS OF PREY
1 Most of the letters in "whack" are here.

WORD LIST 58: ON THE CUTTING EDGE
1 Word before buck, dust, or mill.

WORD LIST 59: WORDS WITH X IN THEM
1 Cat with tufted ears.

WORD LIST 60: PIES
1 Dangerous gift for Snow White.

WORD LIST 61: OUTER SPACE
1 It's a cleanser.

WORD LIST 62: NONSENSE!
1 Here's a hint: it isn't "gooey."

WORD LIST 63: IN THE TOOLSHED
1 Any old feller would have one of these.

WORD LIST 64: WORDS WITH C IN THEM
1 Z works here.

WORD LIST 65: WORLD RIVERS
1 River through ten countries of Africa.

WORD LIST 66: SHALL WE DANCE?
1 Try the J in this word.

WORD LIST 67: WORDS WITH P IN THEM
1 Five of the letters in "opiate" are here.

WORD LIST 68: ASIAN COUNTRIES
1 The S ends up in this Mekong River nation.

WORD LIST 69: HATS
1 Two of the solo letters surround the E here.

WORD LIST 70: BOARD GAMES
1 Whodunit item.

WORD LIST 71: THE V-8 EIGHT
1 Get your "B" veggie here.

WORD LIST 72: AT THE CIRCUS
1 What tamers try to tame.

WORD LIST 73: **PASTA**
1 The Z goes here.

WORD LIST 74: **WORDS WITH M IN THEM**
1 We can't explain it—it's just something in the air.

WORD LIST 75: **PARDON MY FRENCH**
1 Here's a hint: say "duh!"

WORD LIST 76: **TIMBER TIME**
1 Hint: It's not oaf, oar, or oat.

WORD LIST 77: **WORDS WITH Z IN THEM**
1 Kind of code.

WORD LIST 78: **BROADWAY MUSICALS**
1 This play had legs—and whiskers.

WORD LIST 79: **HOUSE STYLES**
1 Know your ABC's? Use all three in this word.

WORD LIST 80: **WORDS WITH J IN THEM**
1 Place actress Gardner's first name and have a cuppa.

WORD LIST 81: **IN THE TOY BOX**
1 You might OPT to spin some letters around.

WORD LIST 82: **WINE-Y WORDS**
1 Stumped? Try the letters in OKAY.

WORD LIST 83: **THE WILD, WILD WEST**
1 Type of dressing.

WORD LIST 84: **WORDS WITH W IN THEM**
1 You'd be right to be WARY, but mix 'em up a little.

WORD LIST 85: **SCARY CREATURES**
1 Belfry critters.

WORD LIST 86: **BOGUS**
1 Two solo letters surround the U. It could be a kind of rap.

WORD LIST 87: **WORDS WITH U IN THEM**
1 Sound that a B makes.

WORD LIST 88: **A HORSE, OF COURSE**
1 Florida's Biscayne ___

WORD LIST 89: **WHERE THE WHITE THINGS ARE**
1 Starts with M.

WORD LIST 90: **THINGS FROM CHINA**
1 Last three letters are something cold to the touch.

WORD LIST 91: **THINGS THAT ARE GREEN**
1 Try the J here.

WORD LIST 92: **WORDS WITH H IN THEM**
1 This is the X word; that should narrow it down!

WORD LIST 93: **TRADEMARKS**
1 Need a heat-resistant glass? Here's your answer.

WORD LIST 94: **WORDS WITH TWO Y's**
1 Start here with the F.

WORD LIST 95: **JAIL, TO A JAILBIRD**
1 What not to do if you're making James Bond a martini.

WORD LIST 96: **WORDS THAT START WITH I**
1 Hint: there's no K, so no, it's not IKEA.

WORD LIST 97: U.S. PLACES WITH INDIAN NAMES

1 It preceded *Vice* on a TV show.

WORD LIST 98: WORDS WITH K IN THEM

1 It's a fruit, a bird, a shoe polish. Still stumped? Use the W.

WORD LIST 99: THINGS FROM JAPAN

1 An M fits here.

WORD LIST 100: FIVE-VOWEL WORDS

1 Guess where the Q goes!

WORD LIST 1: THE PLANETS

2 An anagram of HEART.

WORD LIST 2: WORDS THAT START WITH G

2 Where the Z fits.

WORD LIST 3: WAYS TO SAY HI AND BYE

2 It may be followed by "amigo."

WORD LIST 4: WORDS THAT START WITH T

2 Play Atari games? This has those letters.

WORD LIST 5: STAR SIGNS

2 The two missing letters are next to each other in the alphabet.

WORD LIST 6: WORDS THAT START WITH O

2 Desert pit stop.

WORD LIST 7: EUROPEAN COUNTRIES
2 Oops...the F-word?

WORD LIST 8: THEY'RE JUST GEMS!
2 Think Dorothy's slippers.

WORD LIST 9: WORDS THAT START WITH D
2 Hamlet, for example, or a kind of queen.

WORD LIST 10: HAWAII
2 Dance with the same letters as HAUL.

WORD LIST 11: CARD GAMES
2 A "red hot" card game.

WORD LIST 12: WORDS THAT START WITH V
2 It's a word with an F, but not an F-word.

WORD LIST 13: AT THE ZOO
2 The W fits here.

WORD LIST 14: ONE-NAMED SINGERS
2 "Only Time" will tell if you can get her name.

WORD LIST 15: GONE FISHIN'
2 You're on your own here!

WORD LIST 16: BACK TO SCHOOL
2 They're far from spineless!

WORD LIST 17: WORDS WITH Q IN THEM
2 This hint is one of a kind.

WORD LIST 18: MUSICAL INSTRUMENTS
2 One of the B's goes here.

WORD LIST 19: GETTING INTO SHAPES
2 Five of the letters of "shrimp" are in this word.

WORD LIST 20: WORDS THAT START WITH E
2 The W is here.

WORD LIST 21: DINING AT A DINER
2 Someone in the kitchen.

WORD LIST 22: BOATS
2 It's an anagram of OCEAN.

WORD LIST 23: SOUTH AMERICAN COUNTRIES
2 Starts with C.

WORD LIST 24: KITCHEN PLUG-INS
2 It could be a potbelly.

WORD LIST 25: WORDS THAT START WITH N
2 Refit a HINGE here.

WORD LIST 26: IT'S A BIRD!
2 One of the B's goes here.

WORD LIST 27: MONEY SLANG
2 Cousins of mussels.

WORD LIST 28: GREEN ___
2 One of five.

WORD LIST 29: TREE'S COMPANY
2 Need needles? This tree can help.

WORD LIST 30: WORDS THAT START WITH A
2 One of the X's works here.

WORD LIST 31: ___ HORSE

2 The F goes here somewhere.

WORD LIST 32: MOUNTAINS

2 An F opens this Honshu volcano.

WORD LIST 33: THE SPACE RACE

2 Program that made the first manned flight to the Moon.

WORD LIST 34: MEN IN SMOCKS

2 The start of a count is in the middle.

WORD LIST 35: WORDS THAT START WITH R

2 Safari sight.

WORD LIST 36: BAKERY BUYS

2 Bakery buy for Clark GABLE, rearranged a bit.

WORD LIST 37: LANGUAGES

2 The F goes here.

WORD LIST 38: SCHOOL SUBJECTS

2 Word before "lover" or after "pig."

WORD LIST 39: WORDS THAT START WITH Y

2 Japanese currency can lead you to a busybody.

WORD LIST 40: MUSICAL GENRES

2 Read backwards, it's the norm on a golf course.

WORD LIST 41: WINE LIST

2 Wine sold by a CARTEL? At least it has those letters.

WORD LIST 42: DOWN UNDER

2 Eucalyptus-leaf lover.

WORD LIST 43: **WORDS THAT START WITH B**
2 V works here.

WORD LIST 44: **EXPLORERS**
2 The K appears here.

WORD LIST 45: **OSCAR-WINNING MOVIES**
2 Remove the second letter and you've got money left.

WORD LIST 46: **WORDS THAT START WITH S**
2 In a lather.

WORD LIST 47: **LET US PRAY**
2 Two of the H's fit here.

WORD LIST 48: **POPULAR PASTIMES**
2 Starts with C.

WORD LIST 49: **COLLEGES**
2 Jodie Foster's alma mater.

WORD LIST 50: **WORDS WITH F IN THEM**
2 We challenge you to put the D here.

WORD LIST 51: **CARTOON DOGS**
2 Disney cocker spaniel whose name starts with L.

WORD LIST 52: **AFRICAN COUNTRIES**
2 Starts with G.

WORD LIST 53: **THEY COME IN PAIRS**
2 They go on one leg at a time.

WORD LIST 54: **WORDS THAT START WITH L**
2 Hand-held harp.

WORD LIST 55: DOCTOR WHO?

2 Ends in K.

WORD LIST 56: BLUE ___

2 After blue, it means an aristocrat.

WORD LIST 57: BIRDS OF PREY

2 You can watch this one fly, or go fly one yourself.

WORD LIST 58: ON THE CUTTING EDGE

2 Here's where the Z lives.

WORD LIST 59: WORDS WITH X IN THEM

2 It's fair to say there's a P in here.

WORD LIST 60: PIES

2 Same letters as in CHEAP.

WORD LIST 61: OUTER SPACE

2 Think Carl Sagan's PBS series.

WORD LIST 62: NONSENSE!

2 Insect that doesn't know the words?

WORD LIST 63: IN THE TOOLSHED

2 Remove the second letter and you've got a kind of pickle.

WORD LIST 64: WORDS WITH C IN THEM

2 Uses five of the letters in "romance."

WORD LIST 65: WORLD RIVERS

2 Use the C and think of a Crichton novel.

WORD LIST 66: SHALL WE DANCE?

2 Santa's laugh starts this one.

WORD LIST 67: WORDS WITH P IN THEM
2 A place to find privacy, though not with AC.

WORD LIST 68: ASIAN COUNTRIES
2 The home of Confucius also means the good tableware.

WORD LIST 69: HATS
2 Word that can follow "roller" or "demolition."

WORD LIST 70: BOARD GAMES
2 Rearrange IRKS for a game of world conquest.

WORD LIST 71: THE V-8 EIGHT
2 Crunchy stalk.

WORD LIST 72: AT THE CIRCUS
2 Krusty and Bozo, e.g.

WORD LIST 73: PASTA
2 Five of these letters are found in "pennies."

WORD LIST 74: WORDS WITH M IN THEM
2 Where'd that mixed-up BUM GO? To get some Cajun stew.

WORD LIST 75: PARDON MY FRENCH
2 The B works here.

WORD LIST 76: TIMBER TIME
2 Starts with a three-letter word for a Cleopatra biter.

WORD LIST 77: WORDS WITH Z IN THEM
2 The only B is here.

WORD LIST 78: BROADWAY MUSICALS
2 Synonym for "torn."

WORD LIST 79: HOUSE STYLES

2 Domed domicile.

WORD LIST 80: WORDS WITH J IN THEM

2 Don't let this dojo sport throw you!

WORD LIST 81: IN THE TOY BOX

2 OGLE the G for these interlocking plastic bricks.

WORD LIST 82: WINE-Y WORDS

2 Starts with C.

WORD LIST 83: THE WILD, WILD WEST

2 The P works here.

WORD LIST 84: WORDS WITH W IN THEM

2 Four of the letters in "women" appear here.

WORD LIST 85: SCARY CREATURES

2 House haunter.

WORD LIST 86: BOGUS

2 The K works here.

WORD LIST 87: WORDS WITH U IN THEM

2 One Z goes here.

WORD LIST 88: A HORSE, OF COURSE

2 Pinta? Inapt? It uses those letters, anyway.

WORD LIST 89: WHERE THE WHITE THINGS ARE

2 Pretzel topper.

WORD LIST 90: THINGS FROM CHINA

2 Grass that tries to scare you at the end?

WORD LIST 91: THINGS THAT ARE GREEN

2 Rhymes with "hint."

WORD LIST 92: WORDS WITH H IN THEM

2 Starts with S.

WORD LIST 93: TRADEMARKS

2 Look in your laundry room for a hint.

WORD LIST 94: WORDS WITH TWO Y's

2 The two halves of this word rhyme.

WORD LIST 95: JAIL, TO A JAILBIRD

2 Remove the first letter to get part of a chain.

WORD LIST 96: WORDS THAT START WITH I

2 Feeling "jinxed"? Remove the J and rearrange what's left.

WORD LIST 97: U.S. PLACES WITH INDIAN NAMES

2 Home of movie stars—and one of the L's.

WORD LIST 98: WORDS WITH K IN THEM

2 The M appears in this notion of cosmic payback.

WORD LIST 99: THINGS FROM JAPAN

2 This food has four of the letters of SHUNS.

WORD LIST 100: FIVE-VOWEL WORDS

2 The G goes here.

WORD LIST 1: THE PLANETS

3 The planet that starts with a V.

WORD LIST 2: WORDS THAT START WITH G

3 Starts with a four-letter word for billy or kid.

WORD LIST 3: WAYS TO SAY HI AND BYE

3 Rearrange A HALO for this.

WORD LIST 4: WORDS THAT START WITH T

3 L fits here.

WORD LIST 5: STAR SIGNS

3 Put the V at the beginning of this one.

WORD LIST 6: WORDS THAT START WITH O

3 The first letter of Greece is here—and also the last.

WORD LIST 7: EUROPEAN COUNTRIES

3 Sounds like a John Travolta movie.

WORD LIST 8: THEY'RE JUST GEMS!

3 Like waves of grain in a song.

WORD LIST 9: WORDS THAT START WITH D

3 Plant the H here and see what flowers.

WORD LIST 10: HAWAII

3 These say "welcome" in Honolulu.

WORD LIST 11: CARD GAMES

3 Two of the solo letters work here.

WORD LIST 12: WORDS THAT START WITH V

3 This has six of the letters in "surveyor."

WORD LIST 13: AT THE ZOO
3 Last three letters spell a thing on a ring.

WORD LIST 14: ONE-NAMED SINGERS
3 This Icelandic singer needs the J, even though it doesn't sound like one.

WORD LIST 15: GONE FISHIN'
3 Ends with S's.

WORD LIST 16: BACK TO SCHOOL
3 The same letter starts and ends this one.

WORD LIST 17: WORDS WITH Q IN THEM
3 The answer? It's a good question.

WORD LIST 18: MUSICAL INSTRUMENTS
3 Instrument you have to sit down to play.

WORD LIST 19: GETTING INTO SHAPES
3 Rearrange CLERIC to get "around" this.

WORD LIST 20: WORDS THAT START WITH E
3 It gives you a way in.

WORD LIST 21: DINING AT A DINER
3 M works here.

WORD LIST 22: BOATS
3 It's a palindromic craft; does that help?

WORD LIST 23: SOUTH AMERICAN COUNTRIES
3 The first three letters will give some people a lift.

WORD LIST 24: KITCHEN PLUG-INS
3 Stir in the B.

WORD LIST 25: **WORDS THAT START WITH N**
3 Get it right and you'll have a queasy feeling.

WORD LIST 26: **IT'S A BIRD!**
3 Maryland's state bird.

WORD LIST 27: **MONEY SLANG**
3 Bakery buy.

WORD LIST 28: **GREEN ___**
3 It starts with B.

WORD LIST 29: **TREE'S COMPANY**
3 Try a B here.

WORD LIST 30: **WORDS THAT START WITH A**
3 Rearrange "A SCUBA" to get this ancient counting device.

WORD LIST 31: **___ HORSE**
3 Two of the H's go here.

WORD LIST 32: **MOUNTAINS**
3 Exodus peak with a no-no in its first three letters.

WORD LIST 33: **THE SPACE RACE**
3 First three letters spell a word for a precious stone.

WORD LIST 34: **MEN IN SMOCKS**
3 First four letters spell a city famous for casinos and divorce.

WORD LIST 35: **WORDS THAT START WITH R**
3 Something in your eye? Yes.

WORD LIST 36: **BAKERY BUYS**
3 Put the first letter at the end for a girl's name.

WORD LIST 37: LANGUAGES

3 Starts with G.

WORD LIST 38: SCHOOL SUBJECTS

3 Ends with a three-letter Victoria's Secret item.

WORD LIST 39: WORDS THAT START WITH Y

3 K appears here; rhymes with "local."

WORD LIST 40: MUSICAL GENRES

3 Satchmo's music.

WORD LIST 41: WINE LIST

3 The M wine.

WORD LIST 42: DOWN UNDER

3 The C works here.

WORD LIST 43: WORDS THAT START WITH B

3 The only word here with two B's.

WORD LIST 44: EXPLORERS

3 The last three letters spell out a constrictor.

WORD LIST 45: OSCAR-WINNING MOVIES

3 Starts with M.

WORD LIST 46: WORDS THAT START WITH S

3 One of the solo letters works here. Guess which?

WORD LIST 47: LET US PRAY

3 What 10-point Scrabble letter usually goes before U?

WORD LIST 48: POPULAR PASTIMES

3 KIN could fit in two places here, but only one makes sense.

WORD LIST 49: COLLEGES
3 College that might give students free toothpaste.

WORD LIST 50: WORDS WITH F IN THEM
3 A little word with a big animal in the middle.

WORD LIST 51: CARTOON DOGS
3 Dog with the same name as a dwarf planet.

WORD LIST 52: AFRICAN COUNTRIES
3 These letters could almost make up a YANKEE.

WORD LIST 53: THEY COME IN PAIRS
3 There's a three-letter gardener's tool in the middle.

WORD LIST 54: WORDS THAT START WITH L
3 The G appears in this word for a chickpea or lentil.

WORD LIST 55: DOCTOR WHO?
3 Mr. Hyde's good side.

WORD LIST 56: BLUE ___
3 Starts with S.

WORD LIST 57: BIRDS OF PREY
3 Bird that isn't really bald, just looks it.

WORD LIST 58: ON THE CUTTING EDGE
3 Excalibur, e.g.

WORD LIST 59: WORDS WITH X IN THEM
3 Glue a P in here.

WORD LIST 60: PIES
3 The middle letter is C.

WORD LIST 61: OUTER SPACE

3 The X goes here.

WORD LIST 62: NONSENSE!

3 Sounds like a word you'd hear at a deli.

WORD LIST 63: IN THE TOOLSHED

3 Ends with P.

WORD LIST 64: WORDS WITH C IN THEM

3 The V word.

WORD LIST 65: WORLD RIVERS

3 The bridge in *A Bridge Too Far* is over this German river.

WORD LIST 66: SHALL WE DANCE?

3 A three-letter first name starts this one.

WORD LIST 67: WORDS WITH P IN THEM

3 Like Shangri-La or Eden, an ideal spot.

WORD LIST 68: ASIAN COUNTRIES

3 The J country—land of sumo.

WORD LIST 69: HATS

3 B works in this skullcap that might have a propeller.

WORD LIST 70: BOARD GAMES

3 Two of the C's fit here.

WORD LIST 71: THE V-8 EIGHT

3 Read as two words, this might mean "auto goes bad."

WORD LIST 72: AT THE CIRCUS

3 That Australian boot brand is hidden here.

WORD LIST 73: **PASTA**
3 Remove first two letters and you have most of a stringed instrument.

WORD LIST 74: **WORDS WITH M IN THEM**
3 This X word has true grit.

WORD LIST 75: **PARDON MY FRENCH**
3 Rearrange ROGUE for this red stuff.

WORD LIST 76: **TIMBER TIME**
3 B works here.

WORD LIST 77: **WORDS WITH Z IN THEM**
3 Go to L for this!

WORD LIST 78: **BROADWAY MUSICALS**
3 The H fits here.

WORD LIST 79: **HOUSE STYLES**
3 This alpine lodge ends with T.

WORD LIST 80: **WORDS WITH J IN THEM**
3 Think Nordic sight that starts with F.

WORD LIST 81: **IN THE TOY BOX**
3 Start with J, then go for onesies or twosies.

WORD LIST 82: **WINE-Y WORDS**
3 Rhymes with "yellow."

WORD LIST 83: **THE WILD, WILD WEST**
3 Use the letters in CLEAT, one of them twice.

WORD LIST 84: **WORDS WITH W IN THEM**
3 Hello. This starts with H, too.

WORD LIST 85: SCARY CREATURES
3 There's a silent H here.

WORD LIST 86: BOGUS
3 Try the letters in FLEAS.

WORD LIST 87: WORDS WITH U IN THEM
3 Starts with F.

WORD LIST 88: A HORSE, OF COURSE
3 Ends with G.

WORD LIST 89: WHERE THE WHITE THINGS ARE
3 One G works here.

WORD LIST 90: THINGS FROM CHINA
3 This symbol of good fortune starts with a D.

WORD LIST 91: THINGS THAT ARE GREEN
3 Pond scum.

WORD LIST 92: WORDS WITH H IN THEM
3 First three letters are a non-PC word for overweight.

WORD LIST 93: TRADEMARKS
3 One of the C's works here.

WORD LIST 94: WORDS WITH TWO Y's
3 The sole C fits here for a sniveling sort.

WORD LIST 95: JAIL, TO A JAILBIRD
3 The J goes here.

WORD LIST 96: WORDS THAT START WITH I
3 The M fits into this popular Chevy model.

WORD LIST 97: U.S. PLACES WITH INDIAN NAMES

8 Sunflower State capital.

WORD LIST 98: WORDS WITH K IN THEM

8 Like a big, heavy parka.

WORD LIST 99: THINGS FROM JAPAN

8 Short Japanese verse.

WORD LIST 100: FIVE-VOWEL WORDS

8 The first five letters spell a side of a diamond.

WORD LIST 1: THE PLANETS

4 Starts with a three-letter word for "took a load off."

WORD LIST 2: WORDS THAT START WITH G

4 Use the L and think, "The puck stops here."

WORD LIST 3: WAYS TO SAY HI AND BYE

4 Words to a blackbird, maybe.

WORD LIST 4: WORDS THAT START WITH T

4 Prom wear.

WORD LIST 5: STAR SIGNS

4 Fishy sign.

WORD LIST 6: WORDS THAT START WITH O

4 The P fits for this fish-loving hawk.

WORD LIST 7: EUROPEAN COUNTRIES
`4` Use the W here.

WORD LIST 8: THEY'RE JUST GEMS!
`4` Ends in L.

WORD LIST 9: WORDS THAT START WITH D
`4` You are fated to use the T here.

WORD LIST 10: HAWAII
`4` Feast your eyes on this gimme!

WORD LIST 11: CARD GAMES
`4` Starts with H.

WORD LIST 12: WORDS THAT START WITH V
`4` How did such a popular flavor ever get to mean "bland"?

WORD LIST 13: AT THE ZOO
`4` You can find six of these letters in "alligator."

WORD LIST 14: ONE-NAMED SINGERS
`4` LIVES, VEILS, EVILS, LEVIS—it's some combination of those letters.

WORD LIST 15: GONE FISHIN'
`4` The letters of TUTOR can help.

WORD LIST 16: BACK TO SCHOOL
`4` This thing with a D might have three rings.

WORD LIST 17: WORDS WITH Q IN THEM
`4` Ingredient in a margarita.

WORD LIST 18: MUSICAL INSTRUMENTS
`4` Take away the first letter and another instrument is left.

WORD LIST 19: GETTING INTO SHAPES

4 To avoid getting HERPES, change the letter sequence.

WORD LIST 20: WORDS THAT START WITH E

4 Mixed-up YALIES can solve this without much trouble.

WORD LIST 21: DINING AT A DINER

4 Starts with a three-letter Halloween shout.

WORD LIST 22: BOATS

4 CATHY might rearrange her name for a ride on this classy cruiser.

WORD LIST 23: SOUTH AMERICAN COUNTRIES

4 The letters of "cedar" fit here, with two more.

WORD LIST 24: KITCHEN PLUG-INS

4 It's ROTATES rearranged.

WORD LIST 25: WORDS THAT START WITH N

4 Last three letters are an old gangster's word for gun.

WORD LIST 26: IT'S A BIRD!

4 Ends in H.

WORD LIST 27: MONEY SLANG

4 Sounds like "...a deer, a female deer."

WORD LIST 28: GREEN ___

4 The H fits here, toward the end.

WORD LIST 29: TREE'S COMPANY

4 Work with AMPLE letters for this.

WORD LIST 30: WORDS THAT START WITH A

4 The first four letters spell the title of a Middle Eastern bigwig.

WORD LIST 31: ___ HORSE
4 P fits here.

WORD LIST 32: MOUNTAINS
4 Two of the R's fit here.

WORD LIST 33: THE SPACE RACE
4 U.S. space station of the 1970s.

WORD LIST 34: MEN IN SMOCKS
4 Try the Z here.

WORD LIST 35: WORDS THAT START WITH R
4 Highly ornate.

WORD LIST 36: BAKERY BUYS
4 Young Girl Scout.

WORD LIST 37: LANGUAGES
4 It's the talk of Taiwan!

WORD LIST 38: SCHOOL SUBJECTS
4 Starts with B.

WORD LIST 39: WORDS THAT START WITH Y
4 Some say it's wasted on the young.

WORD LIST 40: MUSICAL GENRES
4 This word has a K.

WORD LIST 41: WINE LIST
4 ". . . some fava beans and a nice ___," said Dr.Lecter.

WORD LIST 42: DOWN UNDER
4 Joey's parent.

WORD LIST 43: **WORDS THAT START WITH B**

4 One of the Z's is here.

WORD LIST 44: **EXPLORERS**

4 The letters of HOUNDS work here, but not in that order.

WORD LIST 45: **OSCAR-WINNING MOVIES**

4 Stallone flick with five sequels.

WORD LIST 46: **WORDS THAT START WITH S**

4 Fit the HEM in and you're onto our plot.

WORD LIST 47: **LET US PRAY**

4 If you're looking for a clue, you'll find nun here.

WORD LIST 48: **POPULAR PASTIMES**

4 There's a part of your leg toward the end of this word.

WORD LIST 49: **COLLEGES**

4 Remove first letter and get the biggest city in Germany.

WORD LIST 50: **WORDS WITH F IN THEM**

4 A three-letter girl's name ends this.

WORD LIST 51: **CARTOON DOGS**

4 Disney pooch—a non-PC term for "vagrant."

WORD LIST 52: **AFRICAN COUNTRIES**

4 *Raid on Entebbe* setting.

WORD LIST 53: **THEY COME IN PAIRS**

4 Remove first letter and you still have victories.

WORD LIST 54: **WORDS THAT START WITH L**

4 You can find two altar words in the last three letters here.

WORD LIST 55: DOCTOR WHO?
4 It's elementary, my dear—use the W here.

WORD LIST 56: BLUE ___
4 The G works here.

WORD LIST 57: BIRDS OF PREY
4 1975 Redford flick *Three Days of the ___*.

WORD LIST 58: ON THE CUTTING EDGE
4 This B word ends with a three-letter word for a trap for fish.

WORD LIST 59: WORDS WITH X IN THEM
4 One in a cast of thousands.

WORD LIST 60: PIES
4 The two letters between E and Y are the same.

WORD LIST 61: OUTER SPACE
4 UNABLE to rework this? It's the one with a B.

WORD LIST 62: NONSENSE!
4 Begins and ends with H.

WORD LIST 63: IN THE TOOLSHED
4 A V works here.

WORD LIST 64: WORDS WITH C IN THEM
4 Rearrange ICEMAN or CINEMA for this.

WORD LIST 65: WORLD RIVERS
4 Yellowstone National Park is its s-s-s-source.

WORD LIST 66: SHALL WE DANCE?
4 The first four letters, read backwards, spell a little biting insect.

WORD LIST 67: WORDS WITH P IN THEM
4 The Q works in this word for "tangy."

WORD LIST 68: ASIAN COUNTRIES
4 You need a mixed-up PLANE to find this country.

WORD LIST 69: HATS
4 Two of the N's go here.

WORD LIST 70: BOARD GAMES
4 Game that starts with the "kissing disease."

WORD LIST 71: THE V-8 EIGHT
4 BLT ingredient.

WORD LIST 72: AT THE CIRCUS
4 The Z shows up here.

WORD LIST 73: PASTA
4 Garfield's favorite dish.

WORD LIST 74: WORDS WITH M IN THEM
4 Last three letters spell a zodiac zoo member.

WORD LIST 75: PARDON MY FRENCH
4 Last four letters are a word for the heart of an apple.

WORD LIST 76: TIMBER TIME
4 Rearrange the letters in RACED for this.

WORD LIST 77: WORDS WITH Z IN THEM
4 Greenhouse gas.

WORD LIST 78: BROADWAY MUSICALS
4 Rearrange the letters in INANE, since this play isn't that.

WORD LIST 79: HOUSE STYLES

4 The P works here.

WORD LIST 80: WORDS WITH J IN THEM

4 Put the C into this popular Couture.

WORD LIST 81: IN THE TOY BOX

4 There's no X—it just sounds like there is.

WORD LIST 82: WINE-Y WORDS

4 Ends with H.

WORD LIST 83: THE WILD, WILD WEST

4 A famous one was O.K.

WORD LIST 84: WORDS WITH W IN THEM

4 Sounds like Mr. Disney, et al.

WORD LIST 85: SCARY CREATURES

4 Has a sound-alike word which is in this sentence.

WORD LIST 86: BOGUS

4 Like the story of the one that got away.

WORD LIST 87: WORDS WITH U IN THEM

4 Old Mercury or big cat.

WORD LIST 88: A HORSE, OF COURSE

4 Horse that's spotted or blotched with black and white.

WORD LIST 89: WHERE THE WHITE THINGS ARE

4 Gold Medal product.

WORD LIST 90: THINGS FROM CHINA

4 Put an M in here and you'll be heading in the right direction.

WORD LIST 91: THINGS THAT ARE GREEN

4 Starts with G.

WORD LIST 92: WORDS WITH H IN THEM

4 See if you can fit all three B's here.

WORD LIST 93: TRADEMARKS

4 The first four letters spell something you need to go fly a kite.

WORD LIST 94: WORDS WITH TWO Y's

4 Opposite of nobody.

WORD LIST 95: JAIL, TO A JAILBIRD

4 Last three letters spell a sardine can opener.

WORD LIST 96: WORDS THAT START WITH I

4 Word that can follow Alcatraz or Nantucket.

WORD LIST 97: U.S. PLACES WITH INDIAN NAMES

4 Where Frank Sinatra was born.

WORD LIST 98: WORDS WITH K IN THEM

4 Last three letters are a kids' channel in TV listings.

WORD LIST 99: THINGS FROM JAPAN

4 The letters in HIS AGE can help.

WORD LIST 100: FIVE-VOWEL WORDS

4 It starts with H.

>–+ • +–<

WORD LIST 1: THE PLANETS
`5` Planet that's always good for a laugh.

WORD LIST 2: WORDS THAT START WITH G
`5` Drywall material.

WORD LIST 3: WAYS TO SAY HI AND BYE
`5` Remove the first letter and there's still a bunch left!

WORD LIST 4: WORDS THAT START WITH T
`5` Starts with a three-letter word for a type of dance.

WORD LIST 5: STAR SIGNS
`5` It's a lot of bull!

WORD LIST 6: WORDS THAT START WITH O
`5` Alas, the ATM here doesn't dispense money.

WORD LIST 7: EUROPEAN COUNTRIES
`5` Latvia's neighbor.

WORD LIST 8: THEY'RE JUST GEMS!
`5` Hitchcock thriller.

WORD LIST 9: WORDS THAT START WITH D
`5` Castle section you don't want to stay in.

WORD LIST 10: HAWAII
`5` A Hawaiian island or a patio space named for it.

WORD LIST 11: CARD GAMES
`5` These letters are the same as in PASSED.

WORD LIST 12: WORDS THAT START WITH V
`5` Two of the T's pop up in this word for a bitter feud.

WORD LIST 13: AT THE ZOO

5 It's spotted in Africa.

WORD LIST 14: ONE-NAMED SINGERS

5 This one ends in G.

WORD LIST 15: GONE FISHIN'

5 Sport-fishing catch.

WORD LIST 16: BACK TO SCHOOL

5 It's often felt on a blackboard.

WORD LIST 17: WORDS WITH Q IN THEM

5 Theroux novel (and Harrison Ford movie) The ___ Coast.

WORD LIST 18: MUSICAL INSTRUMENTS

5 It's a NO at the end.

WORD LIST 19: GETTING INTO SHAPES

5 U is often preceded by what letter?

WORD LIST 20: WORDS THAT START WITH E

5 Use the G in this puzzler.

WORD LIST 21: DINING AT A DINER

5 There's a G in this word.

WORD LIST 22: BOATS

5 The W is here. Extra hint: Think Pequod.

WORD LIST 23: SOUTH AMERICAN COUNTRIES

5 Gotta love a gimme!

WORD LIST 24: KITCHEN PLUG-INS

5 Find a four-letter cornfield bird in this word.

WORD LIST 25: **WORDS THAT START WITH N**
5 The D fits in this word that describes Bedouins.

WORD LIST 26: **IT'S A BIRD!**
5 Rearranged, these letters could spell "a pencil."

WORD LIST 27: **MONEY SLANG**
5 Starts with a cow sound.

WORD LIST 28: **GREEN ___**
5 Rings of these are a popular side order.

WORD LIST 29: **TREE'S COMPANY**
5 Brownie ingredient, perhaps.

WORD LIST 30: **WORDS THAT START WITH A**
5 The Z goes here.

WORD LIST 31: **___ HORSE**
5 Wild and wacky.

WORD LIST 32: **MOUNTAINS**
5 The mountain with a V.

WORD LIST 33: **THE SPACE RACE**
5 The K appears in this 1957 satellite that anagrams to STINK UP.

WORD LIST 34: **MEN IN SMOCKS**
5 Starts with M.

WORD LIST 35: **WORDS THAT START WITH R**
5 Like many a vulgar joke.

WORD LIST 36: **BAKERY BUYS**
5 Two of the C's work here.

WORD LIST 37: LANGUAGES

`5` A word for the spin on a cue ball.

WORD LIST 38: SCHOOL SUBJECTS

`5` What this clue ain't got.

WORD LIST 39: WORDS THAT START WITH Y

`5` Dry weather plant that starts out sounding icky.

WORD LIST 40: MUSICAL GENRES

`5` Get "down" with this colorful genre.

WORD LIST 41: WINE LIST

`5` Ends with G.

WORD LIST 42: DOWN UNDER

`5` Egg-laying mammal that ends in S.

WORD LIST 43: WORDS THAT START WITH B

`5` This is the Q word.

WORD LIST 44: EXPLORERS

`5` This Italian navigator was looking for a route to China.

WORD LIST 45: OSCAR-WINNING MOVIES

`5` Rearranged, the four middle letters spell HAND.

WORD LIST 46: WORDS THAT START WITH S

`5` It's just nuts!

WORD LIST 47: LET US PRAY

`5` A five-letter herb starts this word.

WORD LIST 48: POPULAR PASTIMES

`5` It starts with a pigeon call, ends with a royal figure.

WORD LIST 49: COLLEGES
`5` The letters of ALBUM are in here, but not in order.

WORD LIST 50: WORDS WITH F IN THEM
`5` All but two letters of "festival" are here—and it means the same.

WORD LIST 51: CARTOON DOGS
`5` Think "Arf!"

WORD LIST 52: AFRICAN COUNTRIES
`5` "Casablanca" setting.

WORD LIST 53: THEY COME IN PAIRS
`5` Rearrange PERILS to get these.

WORD LIST 54: WORDS THAT START WITH L
`5` Tryst us—er, trust us, there's an S in here.

WORD LIST 55: DOCTOR WHO?
`5` Start with K for a sawbones of early movies, radio, and TV.

WORD LIST 56: BLUE ___
`5` "___ it, da cops!"

WORD LIST 57: BIRDS OF PREY
`5` Classic Ford model of the 1960s.

WORD LIST 58: ON THE CUTTING EDGE
`5` Another word for tomahawk.

WORD LIST 59: WORDS WITH X IN THEM
`5` Think Sitting Bull and Crazy Horse.

WORD LIST 60: PIES
`5` The D ends this one.

WORD LIST 61: OUTER SPACE
5 Heavenly bodies like Earth, etc.

WORD LIST 62: NONSENSE!
5 Remove the last two letters and you're left with a desktop icon.

WORD LIST 63: IN THE TOOLSHED
5 Starts with C (and means "swindle" in slang).

WORD LIST 64: WORDS WITH C IN THEM
5 A word for debacle, bomb, or failure.

WORD LIST 65: WORLD RIVERS
5 Think Wonder Woman, and a river with a Z.

WORD LIST 66: SHALL WE DANCE?
5 This will have you bending over backwards.

WORD LIST 67: WORDS WITH P IN THEM
5 Both M's fit here.

WORD LIST 68: ASIAN COUNTRIES
5 It used to be called Formosa.

WORD LIST 69: HATS
5 A cyclist should wear one.

WORD LIST 70: BOARD GAMES
5 Look for a scuttling crustacean in the name of this word game.

WORD LIST 71: THE V-8 EIGHT
5 Four of the letters in "spiral" can fill the blanks here.

WORD LIST 72: AT THE CIRCUS
5 Night fliers take up half of this word with the B.

WORD LIST 73: **PASTA**
`5` Start with the capital of Latvia.

WORD LIST 74: **WORDS WITH M IN THEM**
`5` What AILS MA? Too much of this deli meat?

WORD LIST 75: **PARDON MY FRENCH**
`5` Starts with M.

WORD LIST 76: **TIMBER TIME**
`5` Evergreen that might be blue.

WORD LIST 77: **WORDS WITH Z IN THEM**
`5` German word for something fake or inferior.

WORD LIST 78: **BROADWAY MUSICALS**
`5` The K is here, in a Turkish word for "fate."

WORD LIST 79: **HOUSE STYLES**
`5` Cheesy house? (Not really.)

WORD LIST 80: **WORDS WITH J IN THEM**
`5` Rainforest cat or Mercedes alternative.

WORD LIST 81: **IN THE TOY BOX**
`5` She really wears mini skirts.

WORD LIST 82: **WINE-Y WORDS**
`5` Like Type-A types.

WORD LIST 83: **THE WILD, WILD WEST**
`5` Jesse James or Josie Wales.

WORD LIST 84: **WORDS WITH W IN THEM**
`5` Where cows graze.

WORD LIST 85: SCARY CREATURES

5 It's a Z-word.

WORD LIST 86: BOGUS

5 Five of the letters of "python" are here.

WORD LIST 87: WORDS WITH U IN THEM

5 The first four letters mean a sudden upset.

WORD LIST 88: A HORSE, OF COURSE

5 A kind of tree or a reddish-brown horse.

WORD LIST 89: WHERE THE WHITE THINGS ARE

5 It's a brand of soap.

WORD LIST 90: THINGS FROM CHINA

5 Take away the first letter and you still have lots left!

WORD LIST 91: THINGS THAT ARE GREEN

5 It's not easy being him.

WORD LIST 92: WORDS WITH H IN THEM

5 Add H to ARCADE, then rearrange for a false pretense.

WORD LIST 93: TRADEMARKS

5 Put the M in the middle.

WORD LIST 94: WORDS WITH TWO Y's

5 Yo, Hef!

WORD LIST 95: JAIL, TO A JAILBIRD

5 Picnic carrier.

WORD LIST 96: WORDS THAT START WITH I

5 Transpose the letters of UNTRIED for this pushy verb.

WORD LIST 97: U.S. PLACES WITH INDIAN NAMES

5 The last letter here? It's the last letter.

WORD LIST 98: WORDS WITH K IN THEM

5 Start with J to get a big payoff.

WORD LIST 99: THINGS FROM JAPAN

5 *The Mikado* costume.

WORD LIST 100: FIVE-VOWEL WORDS

5 It's okay to take a P here.

>-+-• +-<

WORD LIST 1: THE PLANETS

6 Use the J here.

WORD LIST 2: WORDS THAT START WITH G

6 Think "Toys R Us" mascot, Geoffrey the ___.

WORD LIST 3: WAYS TO SAY HI AND BYE

6 Starts with G.

WORD LIST 4: WORDS THAT START WITH T

6 Rearrange OUTSIDE for this word.

WORD LIST 5: STAR SIGNS

6 Try the Q in here.

WORD LIST 6: WORDS THAT START WITH O

6 There's an angle to this.

244

WORD LIST 7: EUROPEAN COUNTRIES

🔢 Was MEG RYAN mixed up when she visited here?

WORD LIST 8: THEY'RE JUST GEMS!

🔢 The same letter starts and ends this one.

WORD LIST 9: WORDS THAT START WITH D

🔢 Rearrange WIRY DAVE for this place that leads to home.

WORD LIST 10: HAWAII

🔢 Start with one of those K's, big guy.

WORD LIST 11: CARD GAMES

🔢 Ends with Nick and Nora's dog.

WORD LIST 12: WORDS THAT START WITH V

🔢 Rearrange BRAVE TIM for this one.

WORD LIST 13: AT THE ZOO

🔢 There's a tiny insect at the end of this big animal.

WORD LIST 14: ONE-NAMED SINGERS

🔢 This seven-Grammy winner can put you in your place.

WORD LIST 15: GONE FISHIN'

🔢 The F goes here.

WORD LIST 16: BACK TO SCHOOL

🔢 Two of the P's go in this word.

WORD LIST 17: WORDS WITH Q IN THEM

🔢 This B word leads to T&A!

WORD LIST 18: MUSICAL INSTRUMENTS

🔢 V will give you a victory here.

WORD LIST 19: GETTING INTO SHAPES

6 Look for the TAG inside this Arlington landmark.

WORD LIST 20: WORDS THAT START WITH E

6 You'll have to stre-e-e-tch to get to the C at the end.

WORD LIST 21: DINING AT A DINER

6 Joe, to some.

WORD LIST 22: BOATS

6 "Old Ironsides" is this type of ship.

WORD LIST 23: SOUTH AMERICAN COUNTRIES

6 The M works here.

WORD LIST 24: KITCHEN PLUG-INS

6 Starts with another word for "plate."

WORD LIST 25: WORDS THAT START WITH N

6 Place the P here to get a word for Lolita.

WORD LIST 26: IT'S A BIRD!

6 Without the O on the end, it's "on fire."

WORD LIST 27: MONEY SLANG

6 Rearrange IRONED for this one.

WORD LIST 28: GREEN ___

6 All the P's go here.

WORD LIST 29: TREE'S COMPANY

6 Pussy ___.

WORD LIST 30: WORDS THAT START WITH A

6 Sea snail considered a delicacy.

WORD LIST 31: ___ HORSE
6 Something you do for fun.

WORD LIST 32: MOUNTAINS
6 The highest peak in California.

WORD LIST 33: THE SPACE RACE
6 Space probe or 1942 Bette Davis film, *Now, ___*.

WORD LIST 34: MEN IN SMOCKS
6 His name includes another word for donkey.

WORD LIST 35: WORDS THAT START WITH R
6 Rearrange CALIPER.

WORD LIST 36: BAKERY BUYS
6 Starts with D.

WORD LIST 37: LANGUAGES
6 Ends with James Bond author Fleming's first name.

WORD LIST 38: SCHOOL SUBJECTS
6 Starts with a three-letter word found on some towels.

WORD LIST 39: WORDS THAT START WITH Y
6 First three letters spell a Thanksgiving staple.

WORD LIST 40: MUSICAL GENRES
6 Try a G or two.

WORD LIST 41: WINE LIST
6 Unlock A RUDE BOX for this French wine.

WORD LIST 42: DOWN UNDER
6 Aborigine word for "creek" and sportswear brand.

WORD LIST 43: WORDS THAT START WITH B
6 It's an anti-tank weapon and a bubble gum brand.

WORD LIST 44: EXPLORERS
6 Use the solo G here.

WORD LIST 45: OSCAR-WINNING MOVIES
6 "Old Blood and Guts."

WORD LIST 46: WORDS THAT START WITH S
6 Where the B is.

WORD LIST 47: LET US PRAY
6 The D goes here; it's a big church.

WORD LIST 48: POPULAR PASTIMES
6 Last four letters are another word for a minor car dent.

WORD LIST 49: COLLEGES
6 First four letters are a man's name, last four a president.

WORD LIST 50: WORDS WITH F IN THEM
6 Puzzle, stump, and baffle are synonyms of this word.

WORD LIST 51: CARTOON DOGS
6 Beagle who sleeps on top of his doghouse.

WORD LIST 52: AFRICAN COUNTRIES
6 The T turns up in this country.

WORD LIST 53: THEY COME IN PAIRS
6 They could be goblets or goggles.

WORD LIST 54: WORDS THAT START WITH L
6 Pour the Q into this one.

WORD LIST 55: **DOCTOR WHO?**
6 The Z works here.

WORD LIST 56: **BLUE ___**
6 Doggie accessory.

WORD LIST 57: **BIRDS OF PREY**
6 One of the K's begins it.

WORD LIST 58: **ON THE CUTTING EDGE**
6 Rearrange TEACH ME to find a bush whacker.

WORD LIST 59: **WORDS WITH X IN THEM**
6 Ends in R.

WORD LIST 60: **PIES**
6 The K fits here.

WORD LIST 61: **OUTER SPACE**
6 This D-word anagrams to RADIO SET.

WORD LIST 62: **NONSENSE!**
6 The first four letters are a Bee Gees name.

WORD LIST 63: **IN THE TOOLSHED**
6 Begins with the name of a women's soccer star.

WORD LIST 64: **WORDS WITH C IN THEM**
6 Put some MEN in here.

WORD LIST 65: **WORLD RIVERS**
6 "Blue" river you can waltz to.

WORD LIST 66: **SHALL WE DANCE?**
6 Four of the letters in PLANK make up this dance.

WORD LIST 67: WORDS WITH P IN THEM
6 Seven letters of "poisoning" are here.

WORD LIST 68: ASIAN COUNTRIES
6 Miss Saigon's homeland.

WORD LIST 69: HATS
6 Jackie Kennedy hat style that ends in X.

WORD LIST 70: BOARD GAMES
6 First five letters are a word that means to make dry or thirsty.

WORD LIST 71: THE V-8 EIGHT
6 This grabs two of the solo letters, H and N.

WORD LIST 72: AT THE CIRCUS
6 Why is UNCLE ICY? He's all mixed up in this teetering prop.

WORD LIST 73: PASTA
6 Favorite of a guy named Alfredo?

WORD LIST 74: WORDS WITH M IN THEM
6 Start with F and get a word for something in the baby aisle.

WORD LIST 75: PARDON MY FRENCH
6 That H might be found in a castle.

WORD LIST 76: TIMBER TIME
6 The L isn't the first or last letter, but it's in there.

WORD LIST 77: WORDS WITH Z IN THEM
6 Fit a TAN in here to get a section of a poem.

WORD LIST 78: BROADWAY MUSICALS
6 Think Liza Minelli.

WORD LIST 79: HOUSE STYLES

6 Starts with M.

WORD LIST 80: WORDS WITH J IN THEM

6 JAM is part of this word, but where?

WORD LIST 81: IN THE TOY BOX

6 The four middle letters are part of a chain.

WORD LIST 82: WINE-Y WORDS

6 The Q works here—guess where.

WORD LIST 83: THE WILD, WILD WEST

6 It ends with a small Australian marsupial.

WORD LIST 84: WORDS WITH W IN THEM

6 The P goes here.

WORD LIST 85: SCARY CREATURES

6 Rearrange MENTORS for this generic baddie.

WORD LIST 86: BOGUS

6 One of the P's is here, but it's silent.

WORD LIST 87: WORDS WITH U IN THEM

6 Try the letters of IMPURE.

WORD LIST 88: A HORSE, OF COURSE

6 Starts with P (Trigger and Mister Ed were this breed).

WORD LIST 89: WHERE THE WHITE THINGS ARE

6 Two P's in this one.

WORD LIST 90: THINGS FROM CHINA

6 Handy stuff if you have a flintlock.

WORD LIST 91: **THINGS THAT ARE GREEN**
6 Starts with a four-letter word for a generic toy.

WORD LIST 92: **WORDS WITH H IN THEM**
6 "Red sky at night, sailor's ___."

WORD LIST 93: **TRADEMARKS**
6 Hot sauce named for a state in Mexico.

WORD LIST 94: **WORDS WITH TWO Y's**
6 Fictional TV town.

WORD LIST 95: **JAIL, TO A JAILBIRD**
6 Four of the letters in "pocket" are here.

WORD LIST 96: **WORDS THAT START WITH I**
6 The V goes here, at least for a period of time.

WORD LIST 97: **U.S. PLACES WITH INDIAN NAMES**
6 The G goes here.

WORD LIST 98: **WORDS WITH K IN THEM**
6 It's handy for checking out a coral reef.

WORD LIST 99: **THINGS FROM JAPAN**
6 Two of the K's work here.

WORD LIST 100: **FIVE-VOWEL WORDS**
6 The X goes here.

>—•—•—•—<

WORD LIST 1: THE PLANETS

7 Car company that put out the Comet model in the 1960s.

WORD LIST 2: WORDS THAT START WITH G

7 Rearrange GET OMENS for this.

WORD LIST 3: WAYS TO SAY HI AND BYE

7 One of the R's goes here.

WORD LIST 4: WORDS THAT START WITH T

7 Deep-fried Japanese dish.

WORD LIST 5: STAR SIGNS

7 This word starts with a five-letter isle and ends with stuff that pops.

WORD LIST 6: WORDS THAT START WITH O

7 Like a well-trained dog.

WORD LIST 7: EUROPEAN COUNTRIES

7 Last three letters spell a guy's honey.

WORD LIST 8: THEY'RE JUST GEMS!

7 Two P's come together here, but sound like an F.

WORD LIST 9: WORDS THAT START WITH D

7 One of the C's fits here, but use some tact.

WORD LIST 10: HAWAII

7 Three of the solo letters fit here.

WORD LIST 11: CARD GAMES

7 Turn the letters in LONE CHIP into a card game.

WORD LIST 12: WORDS THAT START WITH V

7 Napa sight.

WORD LIST 13: **AT THE ZOO**

7 Place the Z and you'll get this one.

WORD LIST 14: **ONE-NAMED SINGERS**

7 Starts with B.

WORD LIST 15: **GONE FISHIN'**

7 Ferocious fish that starts with P.

WORD LIST 16: **BACK TO SCHOOL**

7 A fifth-grader or hiker might have one.

WORD LIST 17: **WORDS WITH Q IN THEM**

7 Start with a G, as in something like a gargoyle.

WORD LIST 18: **MUSICAL INSTRUMENTS**

7 The last four letters are a skeleton part.

WORD LIST 19: **GETTING INTO SHAPES**

7 Altering ALTERING can give you several answers; only one is a shape.

WORD LIST 20: **WORDS THAT START WITH E**

7 Guess where the Q goes.

WORD LIST 21: **DINING AT A DINER**

7 Remix the letters in OUR CENT for this.

WORD LIST 22: **BOATS**

7 The D works here.

WORD LIST 23: **SOUTH AMERICAN COUNTRIES**

7 A GENT in the middle hooks up with a girl at the end.

WORD LIST 24: **KITCHEN PLUG-INS**

7 What you need for that morning cuppa.

WORD LIST 25: WORDS THAT START WITH N

7 Rookie.

WORD LIST 26: IT'S A BIRD!

7 Try the K here.

WORD LIST 27: MONEY SLANG

7 Starts and ends with S.

WORD LIST 28: GREEN ___

7 Aphrodite or Venus, e.g.

WORD LIST 29: TREE'S COMPANY

7 The H starts this one.

WORD LIST 30: WORDS THAT START WITH A

7 The V goes here.

WORD LIST 31: ___ HORSE

7 Threads.

WORD LIST 32: MOUNTAINS

7 Last four letters spell a highway noisemaker.

WORD LIST 33: THE SPACE RACE

7 Rework AROUND EVE for this.

WORD LIST 34: MEN IN SMOCKS

7 Two G's for the painter of Tahitian women.

WORD LIST 35: WORDS THAT START WITH R

7 Both F's here.

WORD LIST 36: BAKERY BUYS

7 Starts with a three-letter word for an afternoon snooze.

WORD LIST 37: LANGUAGES

7 Kind of moss or omelet.

WORD LIST 38: SCHOOL SUBJECTS

7 One of the M's goes here.

WORD LIST 39: WORDS THAT START WITH Y

7 Hard-working farmer, e.g., or a sailor's rank.

WORD LIST 40: MUSICAL GENRES

7 Trinidad style.

WORD LIST 41: WINE LIST

7 The first four letters are a word for a boyfriend.

WORD LIST 42: DOWN UNDER

7 Throw an M in here and it will come to you.

WORD LIST 43: WORDS THAT START WITH B

7 Word for a boastful windbag.

WORD LIST 44: EXPLORERS

7 Got ESP? This name does.

WORD LIST 45: OSCAR-WINNING MOVIES

7 Ends in C.

WORD LIST 46: WORDS THAT START WITH S

7 One of the Great Lakes.

WORD LIST 47: LET US PRAY

7 It's an anagram of OYSTERMAN.

WORD LIST 48: POPULAR PASTIMES

7 It starts with a nickname, ends with an S.

CLUE SECTION

WORD LIST 49: COLLEGES
7 Starts with D.

WORD LIST 50: WORDS WITH F IN THEM
7 Think Pete or Trevi.

WORD LIST 51: CARTOON DOGS
7 "Big Red Dog" of books and TV.

WORD LIST 52: AFRICAN COUNTRIES
7 The letters of BAMBI are found here.

WORD LIST 53: THEY COME IN PAIRS
7 The first three letters spell a hearing aid.

WORD LIST 54: WORDS THAT START WITH L
7 A clarinet, in slang, is called a ___ stick.

WORD LIST 55: DOCTOR WHO?
7 Doctor with a name that makes him sound lazy.

WORD LIST 56: BLUE ___
7 County fair prize.

WORD LIST 57: BIRDS OF PREY
7 If this bird is circling over you, it isn't TRUE LUV.

WORD LIST 58: ON THE CUTTING EDGE
7 Small dagger or heel style.

WORD LIST 59: WORDS WITH X IN THEM
7 G fits in this honeycomb shape.

WORD LIST 60: PIES
7 There's an old song about this gooey pie.

WORD LIST 61: OUTER SPACE
7 The V word. It's all there is.

WORD LIST 62: NONSENSE!
7 All three P's fit here.

WORD LIST 63: IN THE TOOLSHED
7 The J goes here.

WORD LIST 64: WORDS WITH C IN THEM
7 South American constrictor.

WORD LIST 65: WORLD RIVERS
7 Take the C out of MATCHES and rearrange what's left.

WORD LIST 66: SHALL WE DANCE?
7 Rearranged, these letters form a word that means "tiny."

WORD LIST 67: WORDS WITH P IN THEM
7 Start with a three-letter writing instrument.

WORD LIST 68: ASIAN COUNTRIES
7 B fits here.

WORD LIST 69: HATS
7 It's also a drink before bedtime.

WORD LIST 70: BOARD GAMES
7 The G fits in this game with a doubling cube.

WORD LIST 71: THE V-8 EIGHT
7 The last four letters are little piggies.

WORD LIST 72: AT THE CIRCUS
7 Clint Eastwood starred in a 1984 flick of the same name.

WORD LIST 73: PASTA

7 Word before strap or Western.

WORD LIST 74: WORDS WITH M IN THEM

7 It's a scary whopper of a wave.

WORD LIST 75: PARDON MY FRENCH

7 Put a CAR in the heart of this delicacy.

WORD LIST 76: TIMBER TIME

7 California's state tree.

WORD LIST 77: WORDS WITH Z IN THEM

7 Starts with P.

WORD LIST 78: BROADWAY MUSICALS

7 The first five letters spell a caravan creature.

WORD LIST 79: HOUSE STYLES

7 Rearrange "A BLOWGUN" to get this house.

WORD LIST 80: WORDS WITH J IN THEM

7 The solo T appears in this royal title.

WORD LIST 81: IN THE TOY BOX

7 Mixed-up RAMBLES can lead you to a game of aggies and shooters.

WORD LIST 82: WINE-Y WORDS

7 Both V's go here.

WORD LIST 83: THE WILD, WILD WEST

7 K and B fit here, but not necessarily in that order.

WORD LIST 84: WORDS WITH W IN THEM

7 The first four letters spell a New Testament book.

WORD LIST 85: SCARY CREATURES

7 The V goes in this word.

WORD LIST 86: BOGUS

7 Synonym of "make believe."

WORD LIST 87: WORDS WITH U IN THEM

7 The last three letters are a Mai Tai ingredient.

WORD LIST 88: A HORSE, OF COURSE

7 Two more P's fit here.

WORD LIST 89: WHERE THE WHITE THINGS ARE

7 *Titanic* sinker.

WORD LIST 90: THINGS FROM CHINA

7 This word includes HOP and TIC.

WORD LIST 91: THINGS THAT ARE GREEN

7 Former cucumbers.

WORD LIST 92: WORDS WITH H IN THEM

7 Last four letters spell the opposite of heaven.

WORD LIST 93: TRADEMARKS

7 The first three letters tell you how the weasel goes.

WORD LIST 94: WORDS WITH TWO Y's

7 Another word for snoop or buttinsky.

WORD LIST 95: JAIL, TO A JAILBIRD

7 LAM fits into this word.

WORD LIST 96: WORDS THAT START WITH I

7 Adjective for a doting grandma.

WORD LIST 97: U.S. PLACES WITH INDIAN NAMES
7 Two of the N's fit here.

WORD LIST 98: WORDS WITH K IN THEM
7 Riding position, for some.

WORD LIST 99: THINGS FROM JAPAN
7 Its popularity is "in creasing."

WORD LIST 100: FIVE-VOWEL WORDS
7 Jingly thing a gypsy dancing girl might shake.

>──• •──<

WORD LIST 1: THE PLANETS
8 Poseidon's Roman equivalent.

WORD LIST 2: WORDS THAT START WITH G
8 Place to shoot hoops.

WORD LIST 3: WAYS TO SAY HI AND BYE
8 Hmm...the letters of GEE STRING work here.

WORD LIST 4: WORDS THAT START WITH T
8 Stuff one of the X's in here.

WORD LIST 5: STAR SIGNS
8 Sign for Spidey?

WORD LIST 6: WORDS THAT START WITH O
8 Rearrange HORSE CART for this ensemble.

WORD LIST 7: EUROPEAN COUNTRIES

8 The BMX goes here, but not in that order.

WORD LIST 8: THEY'RE JUST GEMS!

8 Put the Q here.

WORD LIST 9: WORDS THAT START WITH D

8 The F works in this helpful mosquito-eater.

WORD LIST 10: HAWAII

8 One letter is used twice in this word.

WORD LIST 11: CARD GAMES

8 A card game for one—or a lonely diamond.

WORD LIST 12: WORDS THAT START WITH V

8 The S is here, as in Isaac Stern.

WORD LIST 13: AT THE ZOO

8 Big beast that's shorter if you call it by its first five letters.

WORD LIST 14: ONE-NAMED SINGERS

8 Her name means "my lady" in Italian.

WORD LIST 15: GONE FISHIN'

8 Starts with a three-letter word for drinking spot.

WORD LIST 16: BACK TO SCHOOL

8 The X fits here.

WORD LIST 17: WORDS WITH Q IN THEM

8 Don't show your face here (but use the D).

WORD LIST 18: MUSICAL INSTRUMENTS

8 Here's where that X goes.

WORD LIST 19: GETTING INTO SHAPES
8 Most flags are this shape.

WORD LIST 20: WORDS THAT START WITH E
8 Use an X to drive out the devil.

WORD LIST 21: DINING AT A DINER
8 Starts with W.

WORD LIST 22: BOATS
8 Starts with S.

WORD LIST 23: SOUTH AMERICAN COUNTRIES
8 Country named for Venice, Italy (hint, hint).

WORD LIST 24: KITCHEN PLUG-INS
8 Site for magnets and photos.

WORD LIST 25: WORDS THAT START WITH N
8 Miss the good old days? Here's your word.

WORD LIST 26: IT'S A BIRD!
8 There's a BIRD in this bird's name.

WORD LIST 27: MONEY SLANG
8 Starts and ends with S.

WORD LIST 28: GREEN ____
8 Camper's light.

WORD LIST 29: TREE'S COMPANY
8 Ends in S.

WORD LIST 30: WORDS THAT START WITH A
8 There's a PEN in this word.

WORD LIST 31: ____ HORSE
8 The N and G end it.

WORD LIST 32: MOUNTAINS
8 JAR fits in here somewhere.

WORD LIST 33: THE SPACE RACE
8 It's also the name of an educational TV "Channel."

WORD LIST 34: MEN IN SMOCKS
8 Archetypal "Renaissance man."

WORD LIST 35: WORDS THAT START WITH R
8 The D goes here, in a word for outlaw.

WORD LIST 36: BAKERY BUYS
8 The two S's go side-by-side here.

WORD LIST 37: LANGUAGES
8 W is the second letter here.

WORD LIST 38: SCHOOL SUBJECTS
8 Start with C, and don't blow us all up.

WORD LIST 39: WORDS THAT START WITH Y
8 The D fits here.

WORD LIST 40: MUSICAL GENRES
8 Here's where the N goes.

WORD LIST 41: WINE LIST
8 Fitting DON in there may help.

WORD LIST 42: DOWN UNDER
8 Coming-of-age journey in the wilderness.

WORD LIST 43: **WORDS THAT START WITH B**

8 The two L's will keep you on your toes here.

WORD LIST 44: **EXPLORERS**

8 In 1998 it briefly became the "sixth Great Lake."

WORD LIST 45: **OSCAR-WINNING MOVIES**

8 Are you really stumped? Use the B in the middle.

WORD LIST 46: **WORDS THAT START WITH S**

8 The L works in this standoff.

WORD LIST 47: **LET US PRAY**

8 The two G's go here.

WORD LIST 48: **POPULAR PASTIMES**

8 Hobby for someone who likes to work with a plot.

WORD LIST 49: **COLLEGES**

8 Ends with a heavy weight.

WORD LIST 50: **WORDS WITH F IN THEM**

8 Feeling rash or reckless? Put the H in this word.

WORD LIST 51: **CARTOON DOGS**

8 Two of the M's go here.

WORD LIST 52: **AFRICAN COUNTRIES**

8 Q works here.

WORD LIST 53: **THEY COME IN PAIRS**

8 Four of the 14 S's go here.

WORD LIST 54: **WORDS THAT START WITH L**

8 The T works here; think Dr. Frankenstein's workplace.

WORD LIST 55: **DOCTOR WHO?**

8 Rearrange the letters in GRAVEL-STONE for a Peter Sellers role.

WORD LIST 56: **BLUE ___**

8 Try a K at the end.

WORD LIST 57: **BIRDS OF PREY**

8 Getting some Z's could help.

WORD LIST 58: **ON THE CUTTING EDGE**

8 Try the two K's side-by-side here.

WORD LIST 59: **WORDS WITH X IN THEM**

8 Instrument whose name means "wooden sound."

WORD LIST 60: **PIES**

8 The two B's are buzzing around this word.

WORD LIST 61: **OUTER SPACE**

8 Looking for stardom? Look no further.

WORD LIST 62: **NONSENSE!**

8 What you might expect to find on the winged steed Pegasus?

WORD LIST 63: **IN THE TOOLSHED**

8 Cocktail for a carpenter?

WORD LIST 64: **WORDS WITH C IN THEM**

8 Caroline Kennedy's pony, once.

WORD LIST 65: **WORLD RIVERS**

8 Huck Finn's river.

WORD LIST 66: **SHALL WE DANCE?**

8 Put a man's name and a heavy weight together for this.

WORD LIST 67: WORDS WITH P IN THEM

8 Symbol of abundance.

WORD LIST 68: ASIAN COUNTRIES

8 Fit the word for frozen rain in here.

WORD LIST 69: HATS

8 South-of-the-border topper.

WORD LIST 70: BOARD GAMES

8 Starts with B.

WORD LIST 71: THE V-8 EIGHT

8 Rearrange WAR SECRETS for this chefs' garnish.

WORD LIST 72: AT THE CIRCUS

8 The one who says, "Ladies and gentlemen, and children of all ages!"

WORD LIST 73: PASTA

8 It begins with a MAN.

WORD LIST 74: WORDS WITH M IN THEM

8 D word. You'll get a bang out of it!

WORD LIST 75: PARDON MY FRENCH

8 Helpful person at a hotel.

WORD LIST 76: TIMBER TIME

8 The tree with the T.

WORD LIST 77: WORDS WITH Z IN THEM

8 Fancy French word for a date.

WORD LIST 78: BROADWAY MUSICALS

8 RIG fits into this word.

WORD LIST 79: HOUSE STYLES

8 This condo style has a HOUSE in it.

WORD LIST 80: WORDS WITH J IN THEM

8 The B works in a hard candy.

WORD LIST 81: IN THE TOY BOX

8 The first three letters are a word before can or Lizzie.

WORD LIST 82: WINE-Y WORDS

8 Robust, or even something like voluptuous.

WORD LIST 83: THE WILD, WILD WEST

8 That D goes at the end.

WORD LIST 84: WORDS WITH W IN THEM

8 LAW fits in there somewhere—but where?

WORD LIST 85: SCARY CREATURES

8 Grotesque figure on a roof.

WORD LIST 86: BOGUS

8 Like a forged painting.

WORD LIST 87: WORDS WITH U IN THEM

8 It's a lulu.

WORD LIST 88: A HORSE, OF COURSE

8 Budweiser's Super Bowl horse.

WORD LIST 89: WHERE THE WHITE THINGS ARE

8 Mythical horse with a horn.

WORD LIST 90: THINGS FROM CHINA

8 Two of the C's work here.

WORD LIST 91: THINGS THAT ARE GREEN

8 Green veggie.

WORD LIST 92: WORDS WITH H IN THEM

8 The M goes here for music to your ears.

WORD LIST 93: TRADEMARKS

8 Starts with V.

WORD LIST 94: WORDS WITH TWO Y's

8 The V works here.

WORD LIST 95: JAIL, TO A JAILBIRD

8 Starts with H.

WORD LIST 96: WORDS THAT START WITH I

8 The C pops up in this word that precedes Gadget or Clouseau.

WORD LIST 97: U.S. PLACES WITH INDIAN NAMES

8 This Florida city ends with a word for soft drink.

WORD LIST 98: WORDS WITH K IN THEM

8 First three letters are a spot on a domino.

WORD LIST 99: THINGS FROM JAPAN

8 Think John Belushi with sword and ponytail.

WORD LIST 100: FIVE-VOWEL WORDS

8 What some boxers' ears look like.

ANSWER SECTION

THE PLANETS

1. MARS
2. EARTH
3. VENUS
4. SATURN
5. URANUS
6. JUPITER
7. MERCURY
8. NEPTUNE

WORDS THAT START WITH G

1. GURU
2. GAUZE
3. GOATEE
4. GOALIE
5. GYPSUM
6. GIRAFFE
7. GEMSTONE
8. GYMNASIUM

WAYS TO SAY HI AND BYE

1. CIAO
2. ADIOS
3. ALOHA
4. BYE-BYE
5. TOODLES
6. GODSPEED
7. SAYONARA
8. GREETINGS

WORDS THAT START WITH T

1. TOFU
2. TIARA
3. TALCUM
4. TUXEDO
5. TAPIOCA
6. TEDIOUS
7. TEMPURA
8. TAXIDERMY

STAR SIGNS

1. LEO
2. ARIES
3. VIRGO
4. PISCES
5. TAURUS
6. AQUARIUS
7. CAPRICORN
8. SCORPIO

WORDS THAT START WITH O

1. ONYX
2. OASIS
3. OMEGA
4. OSPREY
5. OATMEAL
6. OBLIQUE
7. OBEDIENT
8. ORCHESTRA

EUROPEAN COUNTRIES

1. ITALY
2. FRANCE
3. GREECE
4. NORWAY
5. ESTONIA
6. GERMANY
7. PORTUGAL
8. LUXEMBOURG

THEY'RE JUST GEMS!

1. OPAL
2. RUBY
3. AMBER
4. PEARL
5. TOPAZ
6. DIAMOND
7. SAPPHIRE
8. TURQUOISE

ANSWER SECTION

WORDS THAT START WITH D

1. DEUCE
2. DRAMA
3. DAHLIA
4. DESTINY
5. DUNGEON
6. DRIVEWAY
7. DIPLOMACY
8. DRAGONFLY

HAWAII

1. POI
2. HULA
3. LEIS
4. LUAU
5. LANAI
6. KAHUNA
7. SURFING
8. WAIKIKI

CARD GAMES

1. WAR
2. POKER
3. BRIDGE
4. HEARTS
5. SPADES
6. CANASTA
7. PINOCHLE
8. SOLITAIRE

WORDS THAT START WITH V

1. VAGUE
2. VERIFY
3. VOYEUR
4. VANILLA
5. VENDETTA
6. VERBATIM
7. VINEYARD
8. VIRTUOSO

AT THE ZOO

1. BEAR
2. MACAW
3. MONKEY
4. GORILLA
5. LEOPARD
6. ELEPHANT
7. CHIMPANZEE
8. HIPPOPOTAMUS

ONE-NAMED SINGERS

1. CHER
2. ENYA
3. BJORK
4. ELVIS
5. STING
6. USHER
7. BEYONCE
8. MADONNA

GONE FISHIN'

1. COD
2. EEL
3. BASS
4. TROUT
5. MARLIN
6. CATFISH
7. PIRANHA
8. BARRACUDA

BACK TO SCHOOL

1. PEN
2. BOOKS
3. RULER
4. BINDER
5. ERASER
6. LAPTOP
7. BACKPACK
8. LUNCHBOX

WORDS WITH Q IN THEM

1. QUOTA
2. UNIQUE
3. INQUIRY
4. TEQUILA
5. MOSQUITO
6. BURLESQUE
7. GROTESQUE
8. MASQUERADE

MUSICAL INSTRUMENTS

1. HARP
2. TUBA
3. CELLO
4. FLUTE
5. PIANO
6. VIOLIN
7. TROMBONE
8. SAXOPHONE

GETTING INTO SHAPES

1. CUBE
2. PRISM
3. CIRCLE
4. SPHERE
5. SQUARE
6. PENTAGON
7. TRIANGLE
8. RECTANGLE

WORDS THAT START WITH E

1. EBONY
2. ELBOW
3. ENTRY
4. EASILY
5. ENIGMA
6. ELASTIC
7. EQUINOX
8. EXORCISM

DINING AT A DINER

1. PIE
2. COOK
3. MENU
4. BOOTH
5. SUGAR
6. COFFEE
7. COUNTER
8. WAITRESS

BOATS

1. JUNK
2. CANOE
3. KAYAK
4. YACHT
5. WHALER
6. FRIGATE
7. GONDOLA
8. SCHOONER

SOUTH AMERICAN COUNTRIES

1. PERU
2. CHILE
3. BRAZIL
4. ECUADOR
5. URUGUAY
6. COLOMBIA
7. ARGENTINA
8. VENEZUELA

KITCHEN PLUG-INS

1. MIXER
2. STOVE
3. BLENDER
4. TOASTER
5. MICROWAVE
6. DISHWASHER
7. COFFEEMAKER
8. REFRIGERATOR

ANSWER SECTION

WORDS THAT START WITH N

1. NOVA
2. NEIGH
3. NAUSEA
4. NOUGAT
5. NOMADIC
6. NYMPHET
7. NEWCOMER
8. NOSTALGIA

IT'S A BIRD!

1. OWL
2. ROBIN
3. ORIOLE
4. OSTRICH
5. PELICAN
6. FLAMINGO
7. PARAKEET
8. HUMMINGBIRD

MONEY SLANG

1. BUCKS
2. CLAMS
3. BREAD
4. DOUGH
5. MOOLAH
6. DINERO
7. SMACKERS
8. SIMOLEONS

GREEN ___

1. TEA
2. CARD
3. BERET
4. LIGHT
5. ONION
6. PEPPER
7. GODDESS
8. LANTERN

TREE'S COMPANY

1. ELM
2. PINE
3. BEECH
4. MAPLE
5. WALNUT
6. WILLOW
7. HICKORY
8. EUCALYPTUS

WORDS THAT START WITH A

1. AMIGO
2. AXIOM
3. ABACUS
4. AGHAST
5. AZALEA
6. ABALONE
7. AARDVARK
8. APPENDIX

___ HORSE

1. DARK
2. GIFT
3. HIGH
4. PACK
5. CRAZY
6. HOBBY
7. CLOTHES
8. ROCKING

MOUNTAINS

1. ETNA
2. FUJI
3. SINAI
4. ARARAT
5. EVEREST
6. WHITNEY
7. MATTERHORN
8. KILIMANJARO

THE SPACE RACE

1. SOYUZ
2. APOLLO
3. GEMINI
4. SKYLAB
5. SPUTNIK
6. VOYAGER
7. ENDEAVOUR
8. DISCOVERY

MEN IN SMOCKS

1. DALI
2. MONET
3. RENOIR
4. CEZANNE
5. MATISSE
6. PICASSO
7. GAUGUIN
8. MICHELANGELO

WORDS THAT START WITH R

1. RIOT
2. RHINO
3. RETINA
4. ROCOCO
5. RAUNCHY
6. REPLICA
7. RUFFIAN
8. RENEGADE

BAKERY BUYS

1. TART
2. BAGEL
3. ECLAIR
4. BROWNIE
5. CUPCAKE
6. DOUGHNUT
7. NAPOLEON
8. CROISSANT

LANGUAGES

1. ARABIC
2. FRENCH
3. GERMAN
4. CHINESE
5. ENGLISH
6. ITALIAN
7. SPANISH
8. SWAHILI

SCHOOL SUBJECTS

1. ART
2. LATIN
3. ALGEBRA
4. BIOLOGY
5. GRAMMAR
6. HISTORY
7. GEOMETRY
8. CHEMISTRY

WORDS THAT START WITH Y

1. YETI
2. YENTA
3. YOKEL
4. YOUTH
5. YUCCA
6. YAMMER
7. YEOMAN
8. YULETIDE

MUSICAL GENRES

1. BOP
2. RAP
3. JAZZ
4. ROCK
5. BLUES
6. REGGAE
7. CALYPSO
8. COUNTRY

WINE LIST

1. PORT
2. CLARET
3. MERLOT
4. CHIANTI
5. RIESLING
6. BORDEAUX
7. BEAUJOLAIS
8. CHARDONNAY

DOWN UNDER

1. DINGO
2. KOALA
3. OUTBACK
4. KANGAROO
5. PLATYPUS
6. BILLABONG
7. BOOMERANG
8. WALKABOUT

WORDS THAT START WITH B

1. BINGO
2. BRAVO
3. BABOON
4. BAZAAR
5. BAROQUE
6. BAZOOKA
7. BLOWHARD
8. BALLERINA

EXPLORERS

1. CABOT
2. DRAKE
3. BALBOA
4. HUDSON
5. COLUMBUS
6. MAGELLAN
7. VESPUCCI
8. CHAMPLAIN

OSCAR-WINNING MOVIES

1. GIGI
2. CRASH
3. MARTY
4. ROCKY
5. GANDHI
6. PATTON
7. TITANIC
8. CASABLANCA

WORDS THAT START WITH S

1. SAUCY
2. SOAPY
3. SUEDE
4. SCHEME
5. SCREWY
6. SUNBATHE
7. SUPERIOR
8. STALEMATE

LET US PRAY

1. CHAPEL
2. CHURCH
3. MOSQUE
4. CONVENT
5. BASILICA
6. CATHEDRAL
7. MONASTERY
8. SYNAGOGUE

POPULAR PASTIMES

1. GOLF
2. CRAFTS
3. HIKING
4. FISHING
5. COOKING
6. READING
7. BILLIARDS
8. GARDENING

COLLEGES

1. DUKE
2. YALE
3. COLGATE
4. OBERLIN
5. COLUMBIA
6. STANFORD
7. DARTMOUTH
8. PRINCETON

WORDS WITH F IN THEM

1. FLU
2. DEFY
3. FOXY
4. FOAMY
5. FIESTA
6. MYSTIFY
7. FOUNTAIN
8. FOOLHARDY

CARTOON DOGS

1. ODIE
2. LADY
3. PLUTO
4. TRAMP
5. SANDY
6. SNOOPY
7. CLIFFORD
8. MARMADUKE

AFRICAN COUNTRIES

1. MALI
2. GHANA
3. KENYA
4. UGANDA
5. MOROCCO
6. ETHIOPIA
7. ZIMBABWE
8. MOZAMBIQUE

THEY COME IN PAIRS

1. BOOTS
2. PANTS
3. SHOES
4. TWINS
5. PLIERS
6. GLASSES
7. EARRINGS
8. SCISSORS

WORDS THAT START WITH L

1. LAVA
2. LYRE
3. LEGUME
4. LIBIDO
5. LIAISON
6. LIQUEUR
7. LICORICE
8. LABORATORY

DOCTOR WHO?

1. SEUSS
2. SPOCK
3. JEKYLL
4. WATSON
5. KILDARE
6. ZHIVAGO
7. DOLITTLE
8. STRANGELOVE

BLUE ___

1. JEANS
2. BLOOD
3. SKIES
4. ANGELS
5. CHEESE
6. COLLAR
7. RIBBON
8. STREAK

ANSWER SECTION

BIRDS OF PREY
1. HAWK
2. KITE
3. EAGLE
4. CONDOR
5. FALCON
6. KESTREL
7. VULTURE
8. BUZZARD

ON THE CUTTING EDGE
1. SAW
2. RAZOR
3. SWORD
4. BAYONET
5. HATCHET
6. MACHETE
7. STILETTO
8. JACKKNIFE

WORDS WITH X IN THEM
1. LYNX
2. EXPO
3. EPOXY
4. EXTRA
5. SIOUX
6. ELIXIR
7. HEXAGON
8. XYLOPHONE

PIES
1. APPLE
2. PEACH
3. PECAN
4. CHERRY
5. CUSTARD
6. PUMPKIN
7. SHOOFLY
8. BLUEBERRY

OUTER SPACE
1. COMET
2. COSMOS
3. GALAXY
4. NEBULA
5. PLANETS
6. ASTEROID
7. UNIVERSE
8. ASTRONOMY

NONSENSE!
1. HOOEY
2. HUMBUG
3. BALONEY
4. HOGWASH
5. FOLDEROL
6. GIBBERISH
7. POPPYCOCK
8. HORSEFEATHERS

IN THE TOOLSHED
1. AXE
2. DRILL
3. CLAMP
4. LEVEL
5. CHISEL
6. HAMMER
7. JIGSAW
8. SCREWDRIVER

WORDS WITH C IN THEM
1. COZY
2. CAMEO
3. CAVIAR
4. ANEMIC
5. FIASCO
6. FLAMENCO
7. ANACONDA
8. MACARONI

WORLD RIVERS
1. NILE
2. CONGO
3. RHINE
4. SNAKE
5. AMAZON
6. DANUBE
7. THAMES
8. MISSISSIPPI

SHALL WE DANCE?
1. JIG
2. HORA
3. SAMBA
4. TANGO
5. LIMBO
6. POLKA
7. MINUET
8. CHARLESTON

WORDS WITH P IN THEM
1. PATIO
2. PRIVY
3. UTOPIA
4. PIQUANT
5. PREMIUM
6. OPINION
7. PENINSULA
8. CORNUCOPIA

ASIAN COUNTRIES
1. LAOS
2. CHINA
3. JAPAN
4. NEPAL
5. TAIWAN
6. VIETNAM
7. CAMBODIA
8. THAILAND

HATS
1. FEZ
2. DERBY
3. BEANIE
4. BONNET
5. HELMET
6. PILLBOX
7. NIGHTCAP
8. SOMBRERO

BOARD GAMES
1. CLUE
2. RISK
3. CHECKERS
4. MONOPOLY
5. SCRABBLE
6. PARCHEESI
7. BACKGAMMON
8. BATTLESHIP

THE V-8 EIGHT
1. BEETS
2. CELERY
3. CARROTS
4. LETTUCE
5. PARSLEY
6. SPINACH
7. TOMATOES
8. WATERCRESS

AT THE CIRCUS
1. LIONS
2. CLOWNS
3. JUGGLER
4. TRAPEZE
5. ACROBATS
6. UNICYCLE
7. TIGHTROPE
8. RINGMASTER

ANSWER SECTION

PASTA

1. ZITI
2. PENNE
3. RAVIOLI
4. LASAGNA
5. RIGATONI
6. FETTUCINE
7. SPAGHETTI
8. MANICOTTI

WORDS WITH M IN THEM

1. AROMA
2. GUMBO
3. MOXIE
4. SCRAM
5. SALAMI
6. FORMULA
7. TSUNAMI
8. DYNAMITE

PARDON MY FRENCH

1. ADIEU
2. DEBUT
3. ROUGE
4. ENCORE
5. MEMOIR
6. CHATEAU
7. ESCARGOT
8. CONCIERGE

TIMBER TIME

1. OAK
2. ASPEN
3. BIRCH
4. CEDAR
5. SPRUCE
6. POPLAR
7. REDWOOD
8. HAWTHORN

WORDS WITH Z IN THEM

1. ZIP
2. BOZO
3. LAZY
4. OZONE
5. ERSATZ
6. STANZA
7. PIZZAZZ
8. RENDEZVOUS

BROADWAY MUSICALS

1. CATS
2. RENT
3. HAIR
4. ANNIE
5. KISMET
6. CABARET
7. CAMELOT
8. BRIGADOON

HOUSE STYLES

1. CABIN
2. IGLOO
3. CHALET
4. TEEPEE
5. COTTAGE
6. MANSION
7. BUNGALOW
8. TOWNHOUSE

WORDS WITH J IN THEM

1. JAVA
2. JUDO
3. FJORD
4. JUICY
5. JAGUAR
6. PAJAMAS
7. MAJESTY
8. JAWBREAKER

ANSWER SECTION

IN THE TOY BOX

1. TOP
2. LEGOS
3. JACKS
4. BLOCKS
5. BARBIE
6. SLINKY
7. MARBLES
8. TINKERTOYS

WINE-Y WORDS

1. OAKY
2. CRISP
3. MELLOW
4. SMOOTH
5. INTENSE
6. PIQUANT
7. VELVETY
8. FULL-BODIED

THE WILD, WILD WEST

1. RANCH
2. SPURS
3. CATTLE
4. CORRAL
5. OUTLAW
6. BUCKAROO
7. BUNKHOUSE
8. TUMBLEWEED

WORDS WITH W IN THEM

1. AWRY
2. MEOW
3. HOWDY
4. WALTZ
5. MEADOW
6. PLYWOOD
7. LUKEWARM
8. SCALAWAG

SCARY CREATURES

1. BATS
2. GHOST
3. GHOUL
4. WITCH
5. ZOMBIE
6. MONSTER
7. VAMPIRE
8. GARGOYLE

BOGUS

1. BUM
2. FAKE
3. FALSE
4. FISHY
5. PHONY
6. PSEUDO
7. PRETEND
8. COUNTERFEIT

WORDS WITH U IN THEM

1. BUZZ
2. AZURE
3. FAUNA
4. COUGAR
5. COUPON
6. UMPIRE
7. DECORUM
8. HUMDINGER

A HORSE, OF COURSE

1. BAY
2. PAINT
3. MUSTANG
4. PIEBALD
5. CHESTNUT
6. PALOMINO
7. APPALOOSA
8. CLYDESDALE

WHERE THE WHITE THINGS ARE

1. MILK
2. SALT
3. SUGAR
4. FLOUR
5. IVORY
6. PAPER
7. ICEBERG
8. UNICORN

THINGS FROM CHINA

1. RICE
2. BAMBOO
3. DRAGON
4. COMPASS
5. NOODLES
6. GUNPOWDER
7. CHOPSTICKS
8. ACUPUNCTURE

THINGS THAT ARE GREEN

1. JADE
2. MINT
3. ALGAE
4. GRASS
5. KERMIT
6. DOLLAR
7. PICKLES
8. BROCCOLI

WORDS WITH H IN THEM

1. HEX
2. SIGH
3. FATHOM
4. HUBBUB
5. CHARADE
6. DELIGHT
7. SEASHELL
8. SYMPHONY

TRADEMARKS

1. PYREX
2. CLOROX
3. LUCITE
4. WINDEX
5. FORMICA
6. TABASCO
7. POPSICLE
8. VASELINE

WORDS WITH TWO Y's

1. FLYBOY
2. WAYLAY
3. CRYBABY
4. ANYBODY
5. PLAYBOY
6. MAYBERRY
7. BUSYBODY
8. EVERYDAY

JAIL, TO A JAILBIRD

1. STIR
2. CLINK
3. JOINT
4. POKEY
5. COOLER
6. LOCKUP
7. SLAMMER
8. HOOSEGOW

WORDS THAT START WITH I

1. IDEA
2. INDEX
3. IMPALA
4. ISLAND
5. INTRUDE
6. INTERVAL
7. INDULGENT
8. INSPECTOR

U.S. PLACES WITH INDIAN NAMES
1. MIAMI
2. MALIBU
3. TOPEKA
4. HOBOKEN
5. NATCHEZ
6. TUSKEGEE
7. NANTUCKET
8. PENSACOLA

WORDS WITH K IN THEM
1. KIWI
2. KARMA
3. BULKY
4. BEATNIK
5. JACKPOT
6. SNORKEL
7. PIGGYBACK
8. PIPSQUEAK

THINGS FROM JAPAN
1. SUMO
2. SUSHI
3. HAIKU
4. GEISHA
5. KIMONO
6. KARAOKE
7. ORIGAMI
8. SAMURAI

FIVE-VOWEL WORDS
1. SEQUOIA
2. DIALOGUE
3. FACETIOUS
4. HOUSEMAID
5. PNEUMONIA
6. EXHAUSTION
7. TAMBOURINE
8. CAULIFLOWER

THE LAST PAGE

Fellow Bathroom Readers

The fight for good bathroom puzzling should never be taken loosely—we must do our duty and sit firmly for what we believe in, even while the rest of the world is taking potshots at us.

We'll be brief. Now that we've proven we're not simply a flush-in-the-pan, we invite you to take the plunge: Sit Down and Be Counted! To earn a permanent place on the BRI honor roll, just log on to *www.bathroomreader.com*. No join-up fees, monthly minimums or maximums, organized dance parties, quilting bees, solicitors, annoying phone calls (we only have one phone line), spam—or any other canned meat product—to worry about...just the chance to get our fabulous irregular newsletter and discounts on Bathroom Reader products.

You can also send us a letter:

Bathroom Readers' Institute

PO Box 1117

Ashland, OR 97520

Or email us:

mail@bathroomreader.com

Hope you enjoyed the book.

(And if you're skipping to the

end, go back and finish!)